Life
Coaching
for
Work

Life
Coaching
for
Work

*The FORMULA for happiness
and success at work*

Eileen Mulligan

PIATKUS

First published in 2000 by
Judy Piatkus (Publishers) Limited
5 Windmill Street
London W1T 2JA
e-mail: info@piatkus.co.uk

The moral rights of the author have been asserted
A catalogue record for this book is available from the British Library

ISBN 0 7499 1946 9

This book has been printed on paper manufactured with respect for the
environment using wood from managed sustainable resources

Data capture & manipulation by Phoenix Photosetting, Chatham, Kent
Printed and bound in Great Britain by MPG Books, Bodmin, Cornwall

Contents

Acknowledgements

With sincerest thanks to all my clients whose contribution made this book possible.

I would also like to thank Simon Kirby, Maureen Rice for interpreting my words and helping me write this book and Katie Andrews at Piatkus. Finally, thank you Ian for all your love and support, and Patrick James Oliver for your unique inspiration.

Introduction

Most of us have to work, but many of us would do it even if we didn't have to, because work is about far more than just the way we make our living. It can be the way we express ourselves, get a sense of achievement and self-esteem, and also the foundation of our social lives.

Of course, it isn't always easy. Work is not just doing a job, but navigating other personalities and agendas, dealing with all kinds of people and situations, and facing failure and frustration, as well as success and satisfaction too. Stress and burn-out are increasing problems, and many of us will have to deal with them at least some time in our working lives. It makes no difference if you're a chief executive or a new recruit at the bottom of the ladder, your experiences and issues about work are the same. I know, because in my work as a business consultant and life coach, I see people from every kind of job at every level, and I hear the same problems over and over again. A junior solicitor can be under as much pressure to perform as a senior partner. Keeping up with technology can be equally daunting for the shopfloor worker who has to learn to use the latest piece of machinery or the manager who has to purchase and master the best equipment.

▪ Where Are We Now?

One reason for the great increase in the numbers of people with problems in their careers, is the speed of change in the world of work. If you are caught up in the middle of that change or if you are struggling to keep up, it's hardly surprising. A global, 24-hour economy, increased competition, and the attendant growth in pressure to perform, the speed of technological developments and the growth in the 'service' culture have changed the landscape of work almost beyond recognition.

Like many of my clients at all levels, you may be experiencing the side-effects of the new world of work. You may be dealing with increased workloads and responsibilities. Perhaps you have faced relocation. You may have increased or decreased your working hours, or changed from being an employee to self-employed or from a contract worker to a business owner. Or, like many people, you may be under pressure to constantly add to your skills or work within an organisation that is constantly restructuring. There is a wide-felt sense of job insecurity, which is not simply related to the fear of being downsized or made redundant.

In my experience as a life coach, I've found it's not uncommon for people to adopt an insular, heads-down approach in order to cope. It's not that they don't recognise that the world has changed and that they need to adapt to a new, flexible way of thinking of working; their problems come with knowing how to adapt on their own terms. My coaching programme – your Formula for success at work – is specially designed to help you incorporate all of these changes without feeling hijacked and overlooked by your organisation. Through a series of techniques and exercises you'll learn not just how to cope with change, but how to make it work for you. Most importantly, the Formula puts you back in the driving seat of your career. I want to show you just how many choices you have about how, where and why you work. And you will find you have more than you ever realised.

In my role as a business consultant, I find that many companies and organisations often appear to implement change from a very one-dimensional standpoint. They only see how the problem affects them. Ignoring market forces can result in being left behind or becoming obsolete. However, if they fail to account for the implications that change can also have on their employees, they are left with a new problem – a dissatisfied workforce.

Coaching is always about seeing the bigger picture and how the decisions you make affect other people. A coach will often ask you questions, or ask you to look at situations in a completely new way, in order to change your perspective. Sometimes being able to see things differently – whether it's your own situation or somebody else's – can make an incredible difference. Coaching also teaches you that you can *influence* other people, but you can only *change* yourself, and that's where the focus always stays: with you, and with the way you see, manage and resolve different situations. The relationship between employer and employee can only be harmonious when the needs of both are respected and reflected in the decision-making process.

I've experienced many ups and downs in my own working life. Before I became a life coach, I helped to found and run a very successful beauty company. I thought I had my life sorted out – until I found myself paralysed for two months after undergoing spinal surgery – and for the first time began to really examine my life. It was true that my company was doing well and I thrived on it, but my personal life was a mess and my health was wrecked. In fact, from the vantage point of that hospital bed I could see just how out of balance I'd become. I resolved there and then to re-examine all aspects of my life. I knew that I wanted to make changes, and I knew I wanted to make them quickly, but I wasn't sure where to begin or how to make them. And that was how I began to develop my own coaching programme – a programme that worked for me personally and which has been working for my clients ever since.

▪ Life Coaching and Work

Life coaching is a fast, simple, but proven method for turning your life around. What a personal trainer does for your body, a life coach does for the rest of your life. A coach meets with you for an initial face-to-face session to help understand any personal and professional issues that need looking at. Together, you and your coach work out a personalised programme of goals and a strategy for achieving them, and you will either meet or have regular phone conversations with your coach to check on progress, revise the programme, and get solutions and suggestions to keep on taking you forward.

People with work-related issues want coaching because they aren't happy with their job, or because it isn't as satisfying and rewarding as they want it to be, and because it takes up too much of their life to put up with feeling bad about it. If you're frustrated with your own work, or just want to move on and up, you're entitled to take the same view. Many people view 'being happy' at work as an added bonus. I believe it is a fundamental right. Finding the right job, achieving satisfaction and personal success is a life-enhancing – and even life-changing – process. I help my clients to achieve whatever it is they need to make them happy at work with a series of coaching techniques that have proved remarkably powerful and effective. In this book, I want to share this method and my experience with you to enable you to become your own life coach at work.

What Do You Want?

One of the most immediately powerful aspects of coaching is to get you focused on what you want. This comes from identifying your own personal goals, dreams and desires. It moves you away from the common preoccupation of a dissatisfied worker and from becoming too focused on what you *don't* want. The main focus of coaching is what you do want – and in finding ways for you to get it.

Coaching isn't therapy. It doesn't dwell too much on the past or how you got here. The focus is on where you are now and where you want to be in the future. Whether you want to climb the career ladder or step off the treadmill, it's practical, pragmatic and results-oriented, with the focus on finding a solution to a problem. Once learnt, the techniques can be applied in almost any situation. Applied well, I guarantee that they will have a positive effect on your life that will surprise and empower you.

▪ Key Skills and Attitude

I've talked about the difficulties of work and this book is for those people who are not 100 per cent happy with their working life. However, I have, of course, met numerous individuals who are passionate, fulfilled and happy at work, and have also succeeded in achieving a work/life balance.

Now here's a very interesting observation: when it comes to

learning new skills and adapting to change, these individuals have mastered what are often referred to as the 'soft skills'. In a competitive workplace there is a great deal of emphasis on the latest technology and increasing your level of skills. All too often the soft skills, those that are interpersonal and people-oriented, are ignored. These skills are essential. They require you to look at yourself and the way you relate to other people. Coaching will help you:

► change your attitude and approach

► effect lifestyle changes

► understand what's really going on in the workplace

► bring your problems – and their solutions – back to yourself, where you have the power to control them.

The majority of my clients are able to remain in their existing job. Initially, many of them believe the only solution to their problem is to change job or career. It can be a revelation when they discover the level of happiness and success achievable by simply changing their own attitude and approach both to work and the people they work with.

Lifestyle changes will also be a major part of your coaching programme. Work doesn't happen in a vacuum. To achieve complete satisfaction and balance you need to look at every area of your life. For example, work may no longer offer you the sense of community it once did. Technology may be isolating and disconnecting you from other people. You may be communicating through e-mail, the Internet or voice mail, but these don't replace the connection you get from talking directly with another human being.

Throughout this book, you will be using coaching techniques to create the sort of supportive and loving relationships you need, improve your health and well-being, take time – or, more to the point, *make* time – for yourself and sort out your finances.

▪ The Payback of Being Positive

Do you think the secret of happiness and success is having a problem-free life? If this were the secret there would be no happy and successful individuals because I've yet to meet anyone whose life is problem free. If there is a secret, it's being positive. Happy and successful people come in all types, but they all have one thing in common: they are all positive. They are especially positive when it comes to handling problems and setbacks, and that is the key to their success. We're all good at handling the nice things in life – it's the way we handle the tough bits that makes the difference. Think about it – there are lots of brilliant, talented people out there who don't feel happy and successful. Regardless of the highs in their life they can't get over the lows.

I can't tell you why some people choose that option, but what I can tell you is that I do believe it is a choice. You can choose to take a positive approach and to take responsibility for dealing with your problems. And if that's the choice you make it does require you to take action and make changes. Feeling happy and successful is not some future event coming to town like a carnival. You can start your parade today and you have everything you need because you choose when it comes to deciding how you want to deal with your life.

Coaching is not about telling you what to do with your life. My coaching programme, and the Formula I designed to go with it, are there to provide you with a structure. It's a means of getting in touch with the person you are through your values, defining what you want by identifying your goals, and clearing your path by dealing with your problems. I'm not the person who changes your life – you are.

▪ About This Book

A successful economy – and a satisfying career – requires a harmonious relationship between employer and employee. There are lots of business books that purely concern themselves with the very academic nature of business or the economy, and there are lots of self-help books that paint an idealistic image of the world of work that may be far removed from your own experience. The aim of this book is to give you a coaching Formula that encompasses the bigger picture.

By using this Formula you can adapt to the needs of the new

world of work, while taking care of your own needs at the same time. It will show you how to overcome blocks that previously held you back and find a workable solution to any problem.

There will be an overview of what's going on in the workplace and how it affects you. But the Formula for assessing your problems and finding solutions is always brought back to you. You are the centre and focus of this book, and by understanding, challenging and working on yourself, you can affect your situation and the people around you powerfully.

People often give me a lot of background about the work they do, and in particular the people they work with. I hear a lot of armchair psychology about why a particular boss is such a control freak or how a male colleague is having issues with assertive women. The observations you make about those around you can be useful, but it's largely guess-work, and may be based on very inaccurate assumptions. However, the one person you can be truly insightful about is yourself. To make the Formula work, you don't have to apply it to anyone but yourself and your own life.

The Formula for happiness and success can be applied to every aspect of your working life. This book aims to help you whether you are:

► a first-time job seeker

► considering a career change

► returning to work

► experiencing conflict or job insecurity

► struggling to achieve a work/life balance

► wanting to be in charge – you want to be the boss either where you work now or in your own business

► dissatisfied in your current situation because your needs and aspirations have changed and are no longer being met

► looking to be more highly valued – or paid – for what you do

► still looking for the kind of work that will satisfy and fulfil you

► ambitious, and you want promotion and progress.

Maybe at this stage you are not really sure what the problem is. Regardless of your situation, or the problems you currently face, the techniques in this book will give you new and effective ways of dealing with them.

▪ The Formula

Now it's time to learn the Formula for happiness and success at work – a simple, seven-step process that can transform your life. To keep it in the front of your mind, we'll be working with this acronym:

F Focus
O Organise
R Review
M Motivate
U Utilise
L Liberate
A Act

You will be using this Formula throughout the book to discover how to redefine success, set goals, overcome challenges, blocks and problems, change life-long habits, build confidence and self-esteem, and achieve happiness and success at work and in every area of your life. To really make the Formula work for you, carry out the exercises in every chapter, then apply what you have learnt on a practical level. Application is what makes the difference.

Applying the Formula

As you read through each chapter, I will explain how to interpret and use the Formula in various situations. So, for example, let's say you are experiencing confrontation with a work colleague, the Formula works as follows:

Focus

Examine the problem. What is leading to the confrontation? What are the effects on you, your colleague and your work?

Organise

Sort out your thoughts and feelings, which begins by writing them down on paper for clarity. How do you feel about this? How did the situation get to this point? List some possible solutions (never mind how practical they seem at this point – just think of ways it could be resolved). Then give yourself a time-frame for dealing with the problem.

Review

Assess the immediate situation and what you have learnt from it about yourself; review any past or similar experiences; look for patterns; review the information you have acquired; and gain a good general overview of where you are now.

Motivate

Encourage yourself to deal with the problem. You can only do this when you focus on a positive solution and outcome. Think about how you could motivate your colleague as opposed to winning an argument or point scoring.

Utilise

Use your strengths, not your weaknesses. What are you good at? How could you use these strengths to help you with your current difficulty? Ask yourself questions that will move you forward, such as: How can I turn this situation around? How can I make this work for me? What can I learn from this experience? Is there anything I have overlooked?

Liberate

Let go of any limiting beliefs that may be halting your progress. Would a change of attitude set you free from this problem?

Act

Now that you have worked through the rest of the Formula, it's time to take action. Make a list of possible solutions. Decide which is the most appropriate and act on it.

Starting to get the idea?

▪ Facing the Challenge

As an ongoing prompt and reminder to follow through with the Formula you will be asked to 'face' the challenge, which is described in the equation below:

(Formula + Application + Change + Experience) = results

Each time you face the challenge you will be able to record your results and see the progress you are making.

▪ What to Expect

Expect to be pushed beyond your normal limitations. Coaching requires you to be honest with yourself about your strengths, weaknesses and real priorities. That often means re-thinking long-held ideas and perceptions that may have been holding you back, or causing you to take a path you don't really want to follow. For example, many of us end up in jobs we've been conditioned to think are the sort of jobs we ought to want, and we overlook the fact that we may truthfully be happier doing something else.

In order to make the changes they desire my clients commit to the coaching programme. They take responsibility for their lives, redefine their relationship to work and, in many cases, rediscover the person they are beyond their job title. My clients are my points of reference and inspiration for this book, and you will have the opportunity to share their success stories. Like you, they are also experiencing things first hand. The feedback they provide, progress they make and invaluable insights they give, have contributed to this Formula.

▪ Taking Responsibility

The great reward of my work is to watch individuals with incredible potential take responsibility for the problems that stop them fulfilling that potential. You can't believe the speed they make progress at, though of course not everyone moves at the same pace. Coaching is not a soft option. It confronts all of us with stuff we don't like. But its great value – and the underlying message of this book – is to make us realise that no matter what problems or difficulties we face (and we've all got them), it's our responsibility to tackle them.

Responsibility is a positive and empowering thing, so don't confuse it with blame. Finding fault is something most people are very practised at doing. When the trains are running late or we want to make a complaint we want to know who is responsible and whose fault it is. And if you're in the habit of complaining in a way that backs people into a corner, you should be aware that that's exactly what you do with yourself. For example, do you complain by saying things like, this service is disgraceful/ outrageous/you should be ashamed of yourself/you're incompetent? If you do, that's the sort of inner voice you will adopt for yourself when you get something wrong or make a mistake.

Problems become something you beat yourself up with. On the surface you may be blaming others, but ultimately you are the victim of your own thought process. And why go through life in that frame of mind when there is a much better alternative? Here are some useful guidelines to keep in mind when you work through the Formula.

► Always define yourself in a positive way. If you find this difficult use affirmations and repeat them to yourself daily like a mantra. It may feel contrived to begin with because you are the hardest person to convince, but stick with it. It works.

► Watch your terminology – not just what you say about yourself, but what you say about other people.

► Don't predict negative results. You don't know what the Formula can do for you until you try it.

▪ How to Work Through This Programme

As you work your way through this programme, you will be filling in some simple forms. You'll find them at the back of this book in the Appendix. They are simple and straightforward to fill in – but think carefully about your answers before you do (as you work your way through this book you'll find lots of tips and examples to help you). These forms are crucial to the Formula as they help to build a clear picture of where you are and where you want to go, and let you monitor your own progress. The forms and techniques I use in this book are exactly the same ones I use with my clients.

As you work your way through the chapters, here's what to expect:

▶ In Chapter 1, I will begin by showing you the Formula in action and explaining why it will help you achieve happiness and success.

▶ Chapter 2 looks at why you work – what are your personal values and what value do you place on work?

▶ In Chapter 3, I'll be giving you advice on how to go about finding the right job.

▶ Chapter 4 works on understanding company culture – and why it's crucial for your happiness and success that you get to grips with it.

▶ In Chapter 5 I explore whether you can move upwards. Have you got what it takes for promotion or to be in charge? Do you really want to run your own business?

▶ Chapter 6 helps you to develop your communication skills and look at the effective negotiator in action.

▶ In Chapter 7 I look at how to double your income, or learn to market yourself. Are you missing out on opportunities? And do you know what an employer is really looking for?

▶ Chapter 8 is for you if you think the problem lies with the people you work with. Here, I will look at relationships at work and the types of personality you will encounter.

▶ In Chapter 9, I examine power struggles, office politics and competitiveness.

▶ Chapter 10 studies the effects of technology overload and stress. How do you learn to make technology your ally?

► In Chapter 11 I show you how to apply the Formula in the rest of your life and achieve a work/life balance.

It may sound simple, but that doesn't mean it's easy. You have to make a commitment to the Formula, and be willing to take responsibility for applying it.

▪ Will the Formula Work for You?

In short, yes. Maybe you're a little cynical about that claim. Can reading one book really deliver happiness and success in all areas of your working life? The simple and honest answer is: yes it can.

To really benefit from this book you need to read every chapter. In doing so, you'll see that many work-related problems are a knock-on effect of the core problem. When you tackle the effects of a problem rather than the cause, your solutions will always be temporary. Coaching is about achieving fast results, but for those results to be truly effective, you have to be prepared to do your groundwork and uncover your core issues.

Just as the world of work is changing, so is your life. You can continue to revisit this book and apply its techniques, long after your current problems or frustrations are resolved. Good luck!

CHAPTER ONE

The Formula in Action

I CALLED THIS SYSTEM the 'Formula' because when clients come to see me, they are often looking for a magical formula that will transform their lives. They want a way out of their situation, not just an explanation as to why they got into it. So the Formula offers a practical way to move them forwards, and get the results they want. To do that, they have to take action, and so will you.

Taking action is what makes the difference. I can't emphasise that enough. We can analyse problems and even find solutions to them, but if we don't act, we don't move forward. Life is not stationary. You will find your greatest success and happiness by accepting and embracing change, rather than fighting it. If you don't – if you just sit back, feeling miserable as change happens all around you, which it will – you're opting to take a back seat in the journey of your life. My job as your coach is to put you in the driving seat.

Remember the principles of the Formula?

F Focus
O Organise
R Review
M Motivate
U Utilise
L Liberate
A Act

Everything you need is locked inside that simple acronym. It's designed to put you where you need to go: in problem-solving mode, which is what coaching is all about.

Think about your own work problems – the reason you bought this book in the first place. Forget for the time being anyone else you feel is involved in your problem. Your problem begins with you: the way you see it, the way you react to it, and the way you respond to it. Blaming others just keeps you blocked, and your power over them and their behaviour is limited at best. But, what about your power over yourself and your own behaviour? That's as limitless as you want it to be, and that's the key to moving you forward.

The techniques you are about to learn will change the way you look at a problem and that in turn will change the outcome. I guarantee it. With each case history you will see that the Formula always applies the same basic principles. However, depending on your problem and the point you are stuck at, you may need to work through the process more than once to ensure you are using it properly, and to get to an outcome you feel happy with.

▪ Before You Begin

► You need a large A4-size journal, which you will be using for the various exercises. These are included in each chapter and will help you to work through the Formula, relating everything you read in this book directly to you and your situation. Most of the exercises are very simple – they just require that you think hard and honestly about yourself in certain situations – but will enable you to use this book not as a general advice guide, but as a personalised programme for improving your working life.

► Get an A4-size folder, for the coaching forms (see Appendix) and to store information that you will gather along the way.

▪ How Do You Feel?

Before looking at your working life in more detail it's important to establish exactly how you are feeling right now. In Chapter 11 you'll be repeating this exercise, but for the seven key areas of your life, not just work. No matter how important your career, work doesn't exist in a vacuum, so we'll also be looking at how happy you feel with these other areas, and helping to make sure the balance is right.

Circle a number below that reflects your current state. If your working life is making you really unhappy and miserable, give yourself a score of 1. If you are happy with some areas, but not others give yourself a score that reflects your overall feeling.

	Low									*High*
▪ **Work/Career**	1	2	3	4	5	6	7	8	9	10

Now look at the list below and put a tick alongside any of the areas in which you are experiencing problems. This will help you to focus on where the difficulty really lies.

1. Finding the right job ☐

2. Unsure what direction to go in ☐

3. Making enough money ☐

4. Dealing with work colleagues ☐

5. Experiencing job insecurity ☐

6. Lacking in motivation ☐

7. Lack of recognition for the work you do ☐

8. Failure to achieve promotion ☐

9. Feeling bored, not being challenged enough ☐

10. Unsure what skills you should learn ☐

11. Lack of experience ☐

12. Lack of job opportunities ☐

13. A patchy CV or problem with previous employment ☐

14. Afraid to try something new ☐

15. Worried that you have made the wrong career
    choice ☐

16. Would like to be self-employed or have your own
    business, but afraid of the risk ☐

17. Struggling to achieve a work/life balance ☐

18. Unable to adapt to company culture ☐

We will be coming back to this list later in the book. Don't worry if you have ticked several sections. The Formula will help you to identify what the core issue is and what are the related symptoms of the problem.

As I said earlier work doesn't happen in a vacuum, and feeling happy and successful with your work requires you to examine every aspect. So, for example, it could be easy to think you don't like your work, when the reality may be that you don't like the people you work for or with. The problem may not be the nature of your work, but the nature of your environment.

▪ How the Formula Works

Now it's time to look at the Formula in more detail and how you can use it. To take an example, let's say your problem is lack of skills and qualifications.

Focus

This involves focusing on the problem and the effects. It's important to separate the two from each other; lack of promotion may be the effect, whereas the problem is lack of qualifications and skills. Trying to find solutions for the effect is a bit like fire-fighting: there's no point dampening down the flames if the problem keeps reigniting them. So focus on what the problem is and then think about how it affects your work. Write the problem down in your journal because you need to stay clear about it as you work through the Formula.

Organise

First, organise your thoughts and feelings, and write them down in your journal for clarity. Be specific. Use the following headings:

PROBLEM/CAUSE	EFFECTS	FEELINGS
Lack of skills and qualifications	Limited job prospects	Fear of technology
		Low self-esteem
	Being overlooked for promotion	Feeling inadequate

When you are writing down your feelings, name the emotion you are experiencing – I feel angry, upset, frightened, frustrated, disappointed, confused – say it out loud. Give yourself a few minutes here to think about how you really feel. Sometimes the real emotion is masquerading behind the first emotion that comes out. So, for example, the first emotion may be anger, but behind that there is a feeling of upset or fear. Knowing what you are truly feeling allows you to find a better solution. Now list some possible solutions, which tackle the problem. For example, if your problem is feeling stuck in a rut at work, some possible solutions and deadlines might include:

- Increase my skills by the end of the year

- Enrol on a negotiation course before the next salary review

- Register with an employment agency this week

- Research career opportunities in my next week off

It's important to give yourself a deadline otherwise you may have the solution, but fail to implement it.

Review

This can involve reviewing the immediate situation and what you want to do next, or reviewing any past or similar experiences, and looking for patterns. For example, have you failed to get promotion a number of times, in previous jobs as well as this one? If you're honest, have you been avoiding or resisting new technology at work? Do you lack certain skills, either technical or people skills? Maybe you are in conflict with a colleague and this repeats a pattern of finding yourself falling out with people at work, or earlier at school or college? It's important to be honest and try to see the big picture here. It may be hard to do at first, but this is the first step to breaking old patterns and getting the solution you want. The following questions will help you to find out where you are at this point in time.

- What am I trying to achieve?
- How does this situation relate to previous experiences?
- How do I feel about the situation *now*?
- How would I do this differently next time?

Problems can follow you from one workplace to another unless you learn from the experience. Asking the right questions is part of that process.

Motivate

Motivate yourself to deal with the problem. Focusing on a positive solution will help you to stay motivated. Imagine how confident you would feel with new skills and qualifications. Asking the right questions will also move you forward

- How can I turn this situation around?
- How can I make it work for me?

Remember that the focus is on finding a positive solution – not a negative one or a temporary one. An example will illustrate the difference. You have a job interview and part of your job description is to have knowledge of preparing cash-flow projections. You think to yourself – OK, I'm numerate, so I'm sure I can handle this situation when it arises. This is a temporary solution and a negative one because you are assuming you can master skills you don't have. A positive solution is to address the skills you don't have and make sure you get them. That way you will motivate yourself by having the confidence that comes from the experience of having a skill.

It's also important here to consider the position of other people and how you could motivate them – perhaps you need to motivate your boss to send you on a training course? The use of positive affirmations will also keep you in the right frame of mind: 'I'm willing to learn, I want to move forward.'

Utilise

Work on your strengths, not your weaknesses. Lack of skills may be a weakness, but recognising this and doing something about it is a strength. Getting yourself in the right frame of mind is also a strength, so remind yourself that you are willing to learn and are prepared for change. Think about the skills you have learnt to date and how they can be put to use. Remember you are more than a job title; don't overlook your soft skills, which are the interpersonal ones. Identify your special talents in these areas – are you a good listener, trustworthy, reliable and conscientious?

Prepare a skills audit for yourself, listing your hard skills, such as training, education and qualifications, and your soft, interpersonal skills like how you relate to people.

Liberate

Let go of any limiting beliefs that may be holding you back or halting your progress. When you are faced with a problem the emotions you experience have a lot to do with the beliefs you hold. When those emotions are negative ones it's useful to investigate what may be a false belief. Try writing your feelings down on paper, to help you take a more objective view. Fear can cause you to predict a negative outcome to a new situation – 'This is bound to go wrong' – or believe a previous negative experience will repeat itself – 'I'm never popular with management.' When you see the situation in black and white it's much easier to see how old beliefs can actually cause situations like these to occur, and telling yourself that this time things will be different, or that there's a good chance you'll succeed, can make you think and behave differently – and get a more positive result.

Perhaps you performed badly in an interview and therefore believe you are no good in interviews. That's certainly going to affect your future progress. But you can challenge this view. Who says history will repeat? Perhaps you were just badly prepared for the interview. Maybe you walked into the interview in a negative frame of mind. Learn from your mistakes; brush up on effective interview techniques, go in better prepared, improve your frame of mind and discard a limiting belief. Don't remind yourself of what you don't know; remind yourself of what you want to know and learn.

Act

To benefit from finding a solution to a problem you need to take action. This will take many forms. Perhaps you failed to get a promotion and need to ask your boss for feedback on your strengths and weaknesses. Maybe your workplace failed to provide adequate training and your action is requesting it. The bottom line is that until you take action, things are likely to stay the same, patterns will be repeated and the same problems will keep recurring.

▪ Face the Challenge

When you have worked through the Formula it's time to 'face' the challenge, which is described in the equation below:

(**F**ormula + **A**pplication + **C**hange + **E**xperience) = **results**

Formula

The last part of the Formula is Act. I'll explain to you how this is different to what comes next, which is the Application. In order to increase your skills and qualifications you may decide the solution is to enrol on a training course. This is taking action. Now you move onto the application.

Application

The application is the bit in the middle – the doing part of the process. This is where you find yourself on the training course or learning new skills. You may find this a challenge, but coaching is about pushing beyond your normal limitations. Having said that you may well find this immensely enjoyable, because you are on your way. Very often you will have faced a major fear. You may have doubted your ability to learn or absorb information. But the ability to retain information is not just an intellectual or academic process. Interest and passion in any subject helps you to both retain and apply information. True wisdom comes from using and sharing your knowledge. Being selective about how you apply your knowledge will result in you making a limited contribution in the workplace, and could lead to your true potential being overlooked.

Change

This comes after the application. You now have new knowledge, your CV is different, opportunities and choices have expanded, and your previous position has changed, along with how you feel about the situation. Lack of skills and qualifications are no longer a problem. If issues of self-esteem are lurking in the background, those beliefs can be challenged, but be aware that it can take some time to recognise and adapt to your new identity.

> Paul worked his way up, in a major hotel chain, from a porter to a hotel manager. Although he completed various training courses along the way and passed them all with flying colours, he still identified himself with a school report that said, 'Paul would be best suited to manual work as he shows little potential for academic studies.' From this misguided and inaccurate appraisal, Paul spent the next 20 years believing he wasn't very bright. Along the way and despite the growing number of qualifications acquired, Paul had overlooked changing the way he identified himself. The Formula helped Paul to realise that he had been limiting himself by carrying this negative – and false – belief with him. He then used 'face' to help him to get a much more realistic and positive picture of his skills, change his beliefs and to value his achievements.

How you identify yourself is a major part of the process, so don't overlook the changes you will need to make on many levels. It's one thing to be aware of how you could improve yourself in the job market, but quite another to go through life feeling you are never quite good enough.

Experience

This is ongoing. Everyone has a different learning curve. Your experience will be unique to you. Improved self-esteem, confidence, promotion, respect and recognition are all good experiences. If you don't have the desired experience then work through the Formula again to get you to where you need to be. By having an experience you may risk disappointment. But by not having one you can guarantee it. The important factor is that it will always allow you to move forward and make a more informed decision. Along the way you will benefit and learn from the experiences other people have, but remember that what works for one person will not necessarily work for another. It's up to you to create your own experiences and not live through those – be they good or bad – of someone else.

▪ Results

Now you've seen how 'face' works, it's time to record your results. These can include promotion, a pay rise, a new job, increased confidence and efficiency in an existing job. Look for positive results. Don't be dismissive about the results you achieve or fall into the trap of making negative predictions as to how you can use these results in the future.

Tim worked as a personal trainer in a health and fitness club. He came to see me because he was considering taking a sports-injury training course. As with all my clients, I encouraged Tim to focus on his career goals. Much as he loved working as a personal trainer, his sporting passion was football. He liked to define himself as someone who helped other people achieve their personal best.

His dream job was to work with a football club and have direct access to the players. He had a vision to increase his level of skills (i.e. by treating sports injuries) and apply his knowledge as a personal fitness trainer. However, there were some seeds of doubt and Tim needed help organising his thoughts and reviewing his options. When Tim initially made his career choice he considered, what were for him, two equally appealing disciplines, to train as a physiotherapist or a PE teacher. He opted for the latter. After ten years spent in teaching, he became a personal fitness trainer.

During our initial consultation Tim said to me, ' I often wonder if I made the wrong career choice. I could do this sports injury training course, but why bother? Football clubs prefer to work with physiotherapists, the job I'm after doesn't exist.'

I challenged Tim's belief and replied, 'You have a point Tim, why bother doing the training course? In fact I have the same belief about fitness training, why bother? There's all this talk about getting fit for life, as far as I'm concerned fitness trainers are getting you fit for death, as that's the one inevitability in life.'

Tim's response was to hit me with a great argument, as only a committed personal trainer could. 'Have you any idea Eileen what it would be like if everyone shared your belief? Do you know how many people have achieved against the odds, pushed themselves beyond their normal limitations, set new standards and exceeded the boundaries of expectation?' He spoke with passion – an important emotion to get in touch with as it neutralises negativity and breaks down limiting beliefs. I was then able to show Tim the importance of a 'belief system check' and how his own limiting belief could stop *him* setting new standards or exceeding the boundaries of expectation.

Tim re-evaluated his belief and was able to change his former 'why bother' attitude and take action. He did the training course, expanded his experience and the result was he landed his dream job working with a football club and combining his new skills in treating a sports injury and developing an appropriate fitness programme that would not aggravate an injury and allow a player to return to optimum performance much more quickly.

You may also recognise the need to increase your level of skills. In the process you have to take with you your existing achievements and find the best possible way to incorporate them with the new skills you acquire as Tim did. Being dismissive about your achievements and predicting a negative outcome provokes that 'why bother' attitude. I'm sure you're familiar with the expression 'a reality check', well I prefer to give clients what I call 'a belief system check' which often requires some heavy-duty tactics, as I used in my response to Tim. A belief system check is when you question any belief that is stopping you achieving what you want to achieve. This is the time to ask yourself: have I tried all the alternatives? Where is the evidence to say my approach won't work? Do I have the courage to set a precedent? If the opportunity I seek is not presenting itself what can I do to create that opportunity?

Employers will not always explore a different way of working. However, if you don't recognise your own potential, you will never have the opportunity to find out which employers are willing to try. Increasing your skills is a must in today's workplace, but never underestimate your existing skills and the results you have achieved to date.

▪ Getting the Problem Right

If you identify the wrong problem or make it someone else's problem, you won't be able to find a solution. So, for example, if you listed your problem as having a bullying boss, you could very well get stuck with that one, because how are you going to change your boss? Coming at it from that position, you won't. Here are some more examples of how to get the problem right.

WRONG PROBLEM	RIGHT PROBLEM
My colleagues undermine me	I allow myself to be undermined
It's impossible to find good staff	I have a problem recruiting the right staff
If I want a job done well, I have to do it myself	I have a problem delegating work
Whenever I complain at work, it always results in confrontation	I have a problem communicating my needs

As a useful tip, when you write down your dilemma, speak in the first person, so 'I have a problem' as opposed to 'My boss or my colleagues have a problem.' By doing this you will bring the crisis back to you, which is essential to finding a solution.

▪ Using the Formula to Resolve Christine's Problem

I'm now going to take you through the Formula with a client, Christine, who had a bullying boss. Before going into this case history think about a common and serious problem in today's society. Schoolchildren are often the victims of bullies. If your child was being bullied how would you protect him? Much as you would like to jump to his defence and even attack the bully, this won't help your child in the long run. The most important skill you can teach your child is how to counteract the bully. Blaming the school, society or the bully's parents is not useful. Deflecting blame distracts you from finding a solution. That's the point where most people get stuck. We usually see problems as being one way – someone else is the cause of our problems. The Formula works to show you that your problems are all two-way: whatever your problem, you are part of the process that allowed it to occur and it's in your power to resolve it. There is no allocation of blame in this statement. It's simply an acknowledgement of how you got to the position you find yourself in and what you need to do to move forward.

Focus

Christine initially identified her problem as having a bullying boss. She quickly got caught up in telling me how badly he behaved and all the awful things he did. I needed Christine to focus on herself in order to find a solution, so persuaded her to write down, 'I am behaving like a victim.' This made a huge difference as she became able to identify her own reactions and behaviour, which was far more useful.

Organise

Christine then used the following headings to organise her thoughts and feelings:

PROBLEM	**EFFECTS**	**FEELINGS**
Behaving like a victim	Getting bullied	Humiliated
	Becoming incompetent	Anxious
	Constantly whingeing	Stressed
	to other staff	Frustrated
	Not sleeping	Upset

Then she listed some possible solutions: stand up for herself, confront her boss, be less affected by his behaviour, and stop behaving like a victim. Christine needed to keep working through the Formula to find the best solutions. She gave herself a deadline to start dealing with the problem immediately and stop behaving like a victim within a month.

Review

Christine's former boss was a bully, which was why she had left her previous job. Christine was also able to see some very clear patterns in her own behaviour. Her last job had made her fearful about making mistakes and as a result of that, when she started her new job, she was constantly double-checking everything. For the first few weeks her boss had been helpful, but then he started checking up on Christine's work. The more he checked up the more flustered she became and the more mistakes she made. Unintentionally she had given out signals of being incompetent, which is like a red rag for a bully to attack.

This was also a good time for Christine to review her reactions and behaviour. She had become increasingly defensive, which was not a position of strength. Christine reacted to her boss by saying things like 'You are unnerving me', 'I resent that remark', 'I can't work when you keep interrupting me', 'It's not fair – I feel like you are always picking on me.' Of course all these reactions will actively encourage the bully.

Motivate

Christine didn't want to be a victim and was motivated to make the necessary changes. The idea of not having to be constantly defending her position was also appealing. Much as fellow workers were sympathetic, she still felt that they were weary of listening to her constant whinges. I asked her to make a list of adjectives that she would like her work colleagues to use to describe her. Using her list I suggested she look for ways to change her behaviour to reflect these qualities.

Utilise

I asked Christine to make a list of her strengths. These included conscientious, sensitive, hard working, eager to learn, good sense of humour, sociable and reliable. I then asked Christine to identify a particular strength that had really suffered or been suppressed by the bullying. Without hesitation she said 'My sense of humour – I never laugh much at work or make jokes.'

Liberate

I asked Christine to make a list in her journal of the beliefs she would have to hold in order to allow bullying to take place. She believed her boss had the problem and while he did, she was not owning her own part of it, which was responding like a victim. She also believed that one day she would walk into work and everything would be fine. Writing things down has power. In this context Christine could see that her beliefs were not helping her situation, and were contributing to making it worse. Her situation would not just 'resolve itself'. This enabled her to see her own part in the situation, which gave her back a sense of control – if she was part of the problem she could control the solution.

Act

Now it was time for Christine to take action. She made the following notes and action plan in her journal:

- I will not constantly jump into defence mode.

- When my boss criticises me I will ask him how I could improve my work.

- I will respond with good grace and, where appropriate, humour.

- I am going to practise relaxation and breathing techniques so that I feel calmer and my voice sounds less emotional.

- I will set clear boundaries about when I can and can't be interrupted.

- When my boss gives me confusing instructions and information I will ask him to clarify what he means.

A week into Christine's action plan, she rang me to report her progress. Her voice sounded really upbeat, 'I feel like my sense of humour has returned. I'm at least having a lot more fun at work.'

Christine continued to make very good progress. The transformation didn't happen overnight, but was a process of re-education for both Christine and her boss. Christine had to allow some time to adapt to her new identity and way of working in order for her boss to change his attitude and approach towards her. But gradually, Christine grew more assertive and less defensive. She learnt to laugh at herself when it was appropriate, without allowing herself to become a victim of her boss's jokes. They now have a very good working relationship.

Knowing and listing the character traits of a bully won't solve the problem, and dealing with them often requires more than one solution. Reviewing your previous work situations can prove to be very useful. Remember that problems can follow you from one workplace to another if you don't deal with them.

It may seem a rather negative thing to do to define your behaviour as being that of a victim. However, the problem has to be brought back to you and even if you don't like the sound of it, this may be the kick-start you need to change your behaviour. You may not have set out to be a victim, but along the way you may have inadvertently picked up character traits that send out signals to a bully. Bullies rarely change; they just look for new victims. Head for the high ground if you want to motivate yourself, listing positive ways you would like to be perceived and how you can adapt your behaviour to incorporate these.

Remember that humour can be a very good way to deflect an attack from a bully. By that I don't mean self-deprecating humour, whereby you make yourself the butt of a joke. Retaining a sense of humour can stop you overreacting and being overly sensitive.

Losing your sense of humour is a sign of excessive stress. Be aware of this, because retaining it can be a major strength in the workplace.

By working through the Formula Christine was able to 'face' the challenge (see page 10). It's important to note that the application part is an ongoing process when dealing with a bully. This is because they can quickly revert back to unacceptable behaviour. So, while you may not fundamentally change the person, you can change the way they treat you. Christine did this and then experienced a positive relationship with her boss and got the result she desired.

Now you've seen what the Formula can do in practice, it's time to start applying it to your own situation. In the next chapter the focus of this book switches to you, beginning with discovering something you may not have asked yourself fully ever before: why do you work? Before you reply 'for the money' turn to Chapter 2 to uncover your real motivations and requirements.

▪ Coaching Review

► The Formula pushes you into problem-solving mode.

► You are after the best possible outcome.

► A limiting or false belief will hold you back.

► Taking action is what makes the difference.

► You can learn from the experience of others, but that's not the same as having your own experience.

► You have to create your own experiences.

► Bring the problem back to you, if you want to find a solution.

► Be aware of the part you play and how you arrived at a particular situation.

► Keep working through the Formula until you have the experience and results you desire.

▶ Changing your belief means changing your behaviour.

▶ Change the way you react and you will change the way people treat you.

▶ When you have worked through the Formula, remember it's time to 'face' the challenge and then record your results.

CHAPTER TWO

Why Do You Work?

W HY DO YOU WORK? What value do you place on the work that you do? And what do you want to achieve at work – what are your goals? These are the most important questions you can ask yourself about your working life. Understanding your personal values and defining your personal goals are what this chapter is all about. This is where we establish exactly what you really want from work and how you can begin to achieve it.

If you are going to feel happy and fulfilled at work, it should be a place where you can express your real self. But for too many of us the opposite is true – work is the place where we can't be ourselves or where we feel under pressure to be something we're not. Maybe you like to interact with people, discussing all aspects of your work in order to find solutions, but feel that you should appear more self-contained and 'professional'? Or perhaps you love one aspect of your work but not another, yet feel it is this part of the job that is most valued, so it's what you have to focus on.

▪ The Reasons for Working

Study the list below and put a tick next to any of the statements that reflect your attitude and reasons for working.

1. To earn enough money to live ☑

2. To earn a lot of money and enjoy a high standard of living ☑

3. I feel passionate about my chosen career ☑

4. I love the challenge ☑

5. I feel the need to contribute ☐

6. It's a way to relieve boredom ☐

7. I can escape my problems; it's a distraction from facing other issues ☐

8. I'm expected to ☑

9. To gain recognition of being good at what I do ☐

10. To support my family ☐

11. It is a form of self-expression ☐

12. It gives me a sense of community, support and loyalty ☐

13. It's part of my personal development and growth ☑

14. To gain a sense of achievement ☑

15. I want to be successful ☑

16. It makes me feel good and deserving of any gain ☐

17. It provides me with self-respect ☐

18. It gives me status and respect ☑

19. It provides structure and discipline to my life ☑

Chances are you will have ticked more than one statement. Most people certainly need to work for financial security. However, along the way you can get caught up in the day-to-day routine of work and overlook the other reasons. In your journal, list all the statements you have ticked. They will be useful for future reference.

▪ Personal Values

Your relationship with work is a changing one and needs regular re-evaluation. Not only do your needs change, so also can your values. The desire to work is not purely driven by a hungry economy and the need for financial security. Many of my clients have found that a particular career may well have suited them in the past, but it no longer satisfies the person they are today. This can be for a number of reasons. Perhaps you want a calmer working atmosphere. Maybe your work no longer provides the challenge it once did or your workload is stopping you from getting your work/life balance right. Whatever the problem, being clear about your values is fundamental.

We all have values, whether we're conscious of them or not. They underpin the foundation of our lives. If you are clear about them you can make better choices. Even if you get it wrong along the way, as I have certainly done, values provide the springboard to bounce back.

As a teenager, I remember a career officer ticking me off for my flippant attitude towards work and saying, 'You should give some *serious* thought to your future career.' I responded by saying, 'Why can't I give some *fun* thought to it?' That's a sentiment I still hold today, because, while my relationship to and reasons for working have changed, my work-related values haven't. Who said work always has to be serious? With work playing such a dominant role in most people's lives, there has to be a greater link between the person you are at work and the person you are outside work. Trying to leave your real personality at the door on the way in and collecting it at home time puts enormous strain on your emotional, physical and psychological health.

To understand your relationship to work, you need to focus very closely on your true inner self. Think about what is most relevant to you and ask yourself, honestly, what do I value most in life?

How to Assess Your Values

Below you will find a list of common 'life values'. These are the values that you feel are most important to you generally – not just at work. Spend a few minutes reading this list and think about the values you identify with. This list is just a guide, so you can add your own values.

adventure	humour	personal relationships
ambition	independence	power
challenges	integrity	recognition
creativity	learning	religious/spiritual life
family	love	respect
freedom	money	security
friendship	passion	success
health	people	travel
honesty	personal development	trust

Write down those that mean the most to you in your journal. You will be referring to this list throughout the book.

▪ The Formula for Values

I am now going to take you through the Formula for establishing your values.

Focus

Write down in your journal the words 'I value . . .'. Fill in the gap with the values that you feel most apply to you, for example, 'I value my family', 'I value my health', 'I value friendship.' Leave out the word work for the time being. You need to get in touch with your life or core values first, because the two may not be running parallel. I'm not suggesting that work is not a life value, as it definitely is for many people. The aim of this exercise is to find out how your values fit into the workplace. So, for example, if you value relationships, friendship, religious/spiritual life, you need to identify this first and then select a career that allows you to bring these values with you. Working in a ruthless, dog-eat-dog environment would give you a major value conflict.

Organise

Read through the list of values you have made and put them in order of importance. If you value your family above all else put it at the top of your list. It can be difficult prioritising your list and many of my clients have pangs of guilt about putting one thing above another when they feel they have equal importance. However, that's because they are usually trying to separate out the individuals or values that a group heading can cover.

> When Peter, a dentist, was asked to make a list of his values, he thought for a long time before putting his children first and his wife second, but he didn't feel comfortable doing this. He had felt that he had to make a choice between them and, of course, he couldn't. The simple solution was to combine the values, so he put 'family and personal relationships' as his number one value – a truer reflection of his feelings.

Remember that this is a private list for you and it's important that it's a truthful one. Be careful not to put it in the order you think would make other people happy, otherwise it won't work for you.

As you can see from the example below it helps to define your values in more detail.

1. Family and personal relationships – can cover all family members, wife/husband, partner and friends.

2. Achievement and success – can cover every aspect of your life, what you have achieved in your relationships, education, sports, health and so on.

3. Passion – you may be passionate about a creative skill, preserving the environment, a hobby.

Prepare your list of values in a similar way to the above list. Personal interpretation is important; it will give you a blueprint of the person you are, and what really motivates you and makes you tick.

Review

It's useful to review your value list on a regular basis, and in particular when you are experiencing a problem. Instead of getting caught up in the nature of the problem (for example, my boss is always making me work overtime), look to your value list to discover why it is a problem for you. If spending time with your family is a core value for you, long working hours would prevent you from doing this, whereas if finances are your core value the situation may be tolerable for the extra income. Problems are a matter of perception. What you perceive as a problem may not be one for another individual. The values you hold will dictate how the situation affects you.

Motivate

If you have identified your true values, they will inspire you. There has to be a reason for doing things in life, whether that's getting out of bed in the morning, spending hours studying to pass an exam, having children or working in the garden in all weather. Values are your intrinsic motivation. Problems arise when you are in conflict with your values, they are being compromised and when you have lost sight of them. Whenever you feel you're lacking motivation, give yourself a 'value check', to find out what's causing the block. If you are experiencing conflict or stress somewhere, check your list and remind yourself of what is most important to you. Are you trying to ignore those values? Or doing something that contradicts them?

Utilise

Values are your strength. We all have to deal with difficult situations and confrontations sometimes, and values provide the strength and conviction to keep going. It can be easy in the workplace to adopt the values of those around you. However, like an ill-fitting shoe, you will feel the pinch. Just as it would be inappropriate to ignore your own values in your personal relationships, the same applies in a work situation. Here are some examples of how your values can be incorporated into your working life.

VALUE	WORKING IN LINE WITH YOUR VALUES
Honesty	To satisfy this value it may be important to you to be honest at an interview about the skills you have; give truthful feedback; never misrepresent information to clients or customers, even if you are put under pressure to do so; not keep information from colleagues for your own benefit
Passion	To satisfy this value you may have to be doing something you genuinely love doing and have a heartfelt commitment to. You may benefit from a workplace that allows freedom for self-expression and isn't dictated by formal procedure and protocol
Challenge	To satisfy this value you may be happiest in a workplace that provides variety, new opportunities for training, promotion and increasing responsibility

Using your journal, make a list like the above one and next to each value use your own definition of how your values can be utilised at work.

Liberate

This applies to limiting beliefs and values. A value is only limiting when it no longer applies or has any relevance to your own experience. Many of the beliefs you have may be inherited. My own father was a coal-miner and a bit of a rebel. He was very anti-establishment and held the view that the workers were on one side of the fence and the bosses on the other. For many years I accepted his beliefs as factual, until age and experience showed me the disadvantages of drawing a dividing line between the two. It's easy to find evidence to support any belief when you only go looking in one direction. Keep in mind the word 'liberate' every time you feel your values are being compromised. I say this because it's useful to question how you arrived at a particular belief or value. An open mind is a questioning mind, which isn't the same as a doubting mind. Change, especially imposed change (such as many people experience in the workplace), is unsettling. The best way to deal with change is to be flexible. You have to adapt to the circumstances around you without breaking or compromising your true values in the process.

Act

Your actions are there to serve your values. Make sure the two are in sync with each other. Values are your starting point. When you are clear about your values, your behaviour and actions match the values you hold. Never act unless you know your values.

Once you are happy with your list of values, you can use them as a point of reference whenever you work through the Formula. Trying to ignore this list will only lead to future problems. It's amazing how many individuals lose sight of their real values and just drift into a career, without giving much thought to the person they are. You can easily be seduced by what sounds like a good job, but the reality is that if you pick the wrong one it won't feel good. You may want a big salary or a high-status job, but if you have to work in conditions you hate, or in a way that causes you a real value conflict – perhaps treating other people badly or being less than honest – it will always lead to problems.

Jane came to see me because her fellow workers were alienating her. She had landed a well-paid job as a sales representative, with very attractive bonus if monthly targets were reached. However, she soon realised that the company encouraged some very dubious sales tactics. Although the company was careful about not breaching the law, they were definitely breaching Jane's moral code of conduct. She may have been ambitious, but she was also scrupulously honest.

To make matters worse, Jane was openly ridiculed for not adopting company policy. The rest of the sales team was motivated by financial rewards and walking a rather fine line morally posed them no problem. But it posed a problem for Jane, and her first step towards a solution was understanding why.

When she took the job she was attracted by the financial rewards. She was ambitious and felt that a high salary was a measure of her success. I asked her to make a list of her values. Jane undertook this task as honestly and openly as she could. To her own surprise, when she identified her values, she found that honesty and integrity were the highest on her list, followed closely by respect. So, although she had rightly described herself as ambitious and career-focused, she had confused her definitions of success: money was important, but not as important as she'd thought.

Jane realised that it would always be important to her that she had the respect of her fellow workers. In this job, clearly she didn't, and this was what bothered her the most. She was asking herself questions like: Why are they treating me this way? Why don't they like me? Why can't they see things from my point of view? But these questions were keeping her blocked because they were focusing on other people. In order to change the situation Jane needed to focus on her own behaviour.

Jane's fellow workers didn't have a problem with company ethics; she did. Honesty and ethics were crucial values for Jane, but she had found herself in a culture where these values were not highly regarded. When your values are being compromised, you can't throw the problem back on to other people. Jane had been trying to see her unhappiness at work as the 'fault' or 'problem' of her co-workers, an angle that changed nothing, and only made her feel more isolated and miserable.

Once Jane got in touch with her values, it enabled her to see the problem in a new light. On a daily basis she was compromising her beliefs and value system. Jane realised that she wasn't prepared to give up her core values for the sake of financial reward and so she decided to apply for a job with another company. This time she was a lot more careful about her choice and ensured that the company's values reflected her own.

Jane's case is quite an extreme example. Leaving your existing employment is not always necessary. However, if you have initially focused on the wrong values, moving on may be the best way to re-establish a working pattern that is true to your core values and goals.

If you are trying to work out what has gone wrong, asking 'Why' questions, as Jane did, will keep you blocked because they keep you focused on the company's beliefs and other employees' ethics. The

Formula is not about changing other people's values and behaviour, it's about understanding and adapting our own behaviour and taking responsibility for making our own changes. It's far better to ask 'How' or 'What' questions: 'How did this situation arise?'; 'How can I make this situation work for me?'; 'What will make this better?'; 'What can I do to stop this happening again?'. In any work situation, you have to decide how many values you are prepared to have chipped away in order to fit in with the company's attitude. Doing this, however, is often an uneasy compromise and is likely to lead to you feeling dissatisfied with your job.

▪ Integrating Values with Work

Study the following statement:

Do you think it is possible to reconcile your values in the workplace?

People often talk about reconciling their differences. The definition of reconcile means to make two conflicting things compatible. This is possible, of course, but not always. Perhaps you would like to work flexible hours, but this is not an option your employers offer. This could be an acceptable situation if you are happy and fulfilled in the work you do. However, you may not be able to reconcile the difference if you dislike your job or the hours you work create havoc with the rest of your life. The bottom line is that it depends on how the conflict affects you. There is a big difference between reaching a compromise with the values you hold and having them compromised.

If you are experiencing discontent at work, it can be difficult to determine what is a reaction to *change* or a reaction to *values*. Change is unsettling at best, and at worst it can provoke real fear. It's worth noting that even when things change for the better, it can be met with resistance. If you are unsure about what is causing you concern, it helps to give change an incubation period. Allow yourself time to adapt and monitor your reactions. If there is a major value issue at stake, your level of discomfort will remain after the transition. Although a lot of the changes you experience at work are imposed ones, how you adapt to them will be dictated by your values.

EXERCISE

The following exercise will help you see your values in relationship to your work. Look back at the values list you have prepared for yourself.

Take a piece of paper and write two headings at the top: I Have to Work Because and I Choose to Work Because. Now start placing your values under the appropriate headings. For example:

I HAVE TO WORK BECAUSE	I CHOOSE TO WORK BECAUSE
I have to support myself and my family	I want a high standard of living
I have a very high mortgage	I want to have a big house
My children's school fees are very high	I want my children to have a private education
I'm saving up to get married	I want the wedding of my dreams
It's expected of me	I like making my family/partner proud of me
I trained for this job for a long time	I want to use my skills and training

In some cases, a value will appear in both categories. So, for instance, if finances and money are a major value, give some thought to whether this should appear in the 'Have to Work' or 'Choose to Work' category or if it should appear in both. Obviously, it could go under 'Have to Work', because most of us do need to earn money to support ourselves. But the amount of finances you require will depend on the choices you make, so if you choose a high standard of living, you will obviously need the finances to support this, and could place your value under the 'Choose to Work' heading. Choosing to work like this because you want extra money may involve longer working hours, increased responsibility, additional training and extra workloads. If this feels like a heavy sacrifice, you may need to reassess how you have prioritised your values.

Working to support yourself and your family won't necessarily translate into you wanting a high standard of living and in today's housing market having a high mortgage doesn't mean having a big house. What I want you to do is examine how your own personal values influence the choices you make and what part you play in the process. Feeling you have to work and there is no element of choice involved is very dis-empowering. We often have more choices than we realise. So be really honest and take responsibility for how personal choices create your situation.

You can use a short version of the Formula to help you with this exercise.

- **Focus** On why you work and what your values are. Do your values cause you any problems? If so, list them.

- **Organise** List your reasons for having to work and choosing to work.

- **Review** How your relationship to work has changed or how it is at the present time and how you want it to be.

- **Motivate** Ask yourself what is it that would/does inspire you to work.

- **Utilise** List the positive aspects of working, because these are your strengths. Make a list beginning with the statement, 'Work provides me with . . .'. You can include everything from finances, a sense of achievement, mental stimulation to social interaction and discipline.

- **Liberate** Are you holding any limiting beliefs about why you work? Perhaps work is providing you with more than you realised. Maybe you have outgrown some of your values and they are holding you back.

- **Act** Do your actions in relationship to work match your real beliefs and values?

▪ Quality Versus Quantity

We all have different reasons for working, but one we all share is that we are trying to improve the quality of our lives. When you experience *too much* stress and pressure at work, there is a quality/ quantity imbalance. Balancing quality and quantity is an important part of my coaching programme and you will meet the concept again as you work through this book.

When time pressure is a major factor, it's easy to forgo a lot of 'quantity' (of time and energy) in pursuit of 'quality' – getting the things we want that we believe will give us quality of life. Much of our life can be taken up chasing this quality of life – working harder and longer hours for more money, or spending a lot of time searching for the right clothes, cars and furniture. Step back and ask yourself if the end result of all those tasks is really enough to justify the bit in the middle – the effort spent getting to that result.

Achieving something worthwhile means hard work. Unfortunately, it is commonly believed that hard work means unpleasant work – the no pain, no gain theory. So we convince ourselves that to achieve real and worthy benefits like possessions, happiness, success, rewards and pleasures we have to make sacrifices in the process. And, even when we achieve a particular goal or desired outcome, it's a hollow victory, because we have lost so much time, focus, energy and all our other resources in the process of achieving it. Understanding clearly what your goals really are, and what you are willing to do to achieve them is very important, and we'll be looking at how to set goals in more detail later in this chapter. Achieving happiness and success requires you to balance quality with quantity. I'm not suggesting that every minute of your working day will feel like quality time, but the majority of it should. And that's what this Formula is about, because it challenges any belief that says you can't enjoy the time you invest in achieving a goal, as well as the end result.

If work feels like a serious sacrifice or value conflict, you are either doing the wrong thing or doing it for the wrong reasons. If you are passionate about your work it will never feel like an unwelcome chore. Equally, if you are doing it for the right reasons you should never feel compromised about your values. There are other issues that may cause you discontent, even when your reasons and values for working are in place, and I will be looking at those in the chapters that follow. For the time being, focus on why you work and what it would take to achieve a balance between quantity and quality.

Focus

How much of your working day is quality time?

Organise

Make a list with the two headings 'Quantity' and 'Quality'. Then take an average week and list your activities and time spent doing them, under the Quantity heading. Next to this, note how much time is quality time – time when you are really experiencing what you are doing, taking pleasure from it or being very absorbed in it – under the Quality heading. For example:

QUANTITY	QUALITY
40 hours working	10 hours' quality time
28 hours spent watching TV	15 hours' quality viewing
10 hours spent socialising	8 hours' quality time
2 hours spent shopping	10 minutes' quality time

Review

What was your situation like in the past? Did you have more quality time or less? How can you increase your quality time? Use your list to help you with this. For example – if only 15 out of 28 hours spent watching TV are quality time have you slipped into a pattern of numbing out in front of the TV? Is this an old pattern repeating or a new one? If the vast majority of your working week lacks quality time, how long has this situation existed? Can you identify the main reasons why? This is the time to root out any old negative patterns that are repeating and the catalysts for new ones.

Motivate

If you want to stay motivated, focus on the things you like and how you could achieve a well-balanced list. So, remember how good you feel when you have been socialising with people you like or doing an activity you enjoy and make a commitment to increase these hours by freeing up time spent on empty, non-enjoyable socialis-ing. Have more quality working hours by delegating less enjoyable tasks, asking if work you enjoy can be put your way and prioritis-ing what you like doing so you apply for the right sort of job.

Utilise

You can refer to your list for future time management (in Chapter 10), now that you are clearer about the activities you enjoy.

Liberate

Would a change of attitude allow you to have more quality?

Act

What action can you take today to increase your quality time? This could include delegating work you don't enjoy, booking a weekly massage, planning your TV viewing and not overcommit-ting your time.

Now you are ready to 'face' the challenge (see page 10) and do the things and make the changes which will result in more quality time.

▪ Work Goals

I'll be talking a lot about goals during the course of this book, and now is a good time to define goals for the purposes of coaching. Goals are about what you want to get out of life, not a life you want to get out of. A goal should always be positive. It should also be specific.

Here are some useful tips for setting goals:

1. Always write down your goals.

2. Make sure they are in the first person and about *you*:

    ▸ 'I want to be proud of my achievements at work' *not* 'I want my family/partner/friends/colleagues to be proud of what I achieve'

▶ 'I want to feel more valued at work' *not* 'I want my boss to stop undervaluing me'

▶ 'I want to resolve a conflict with my colleague' *not* 'I want my colleague to stop challenging me'

▶ 'I want to contribute more at meetings' *not* 'I want my colleagues to ask me what I think'

▶ 'I want to leave work at a more reasonable time' *not* 'I want my boss to stop being so unreasonable about my working hours'

▶ 'I want more responsibility' *not* 'I want my boss to trust me more.'

3. Goals should be positive. List what you want to achieve, not what you want to eliminate. Don't identify the problem, focus on the desired outcome:

▶ 'I want to earn a pay rise' *not* 'I want to stop being undervalued'

▶ 'I want a new job' *not* 'I want to get out of this rut'

▶ 'I want to increase my skills' *not* 'I want to stop feeling a failure'

▶ 'I want good working relationships' *not* 'I want people to stop picking on me'

▶ 'I want a promotion' *not* 'I want to stop feeling bored.'

4. Set goals that relate to your values. For example:

▶ 'I want to work for a company that values honesty'

▶ 'I want to work in a supportive atmosphere where my personal circumstances are respected'

▶ 'I want to be part of a team'

▶ 'I want to be in a job where my good work is directly rewarded with more money, such as commission.'

5. Contribute to your goal/goals frequently. Keep your list with you and add new goals as you think of them, or

adapt old ones. So, if your goal is to get promoted, you may start to refine the areas you do or don't want to be promoted into, and whether you want the promotion at the company you work for now, or another one.

6. Goals require an action plan. You are not planning to fail – so don't fail to plan. For that promotion, your action plan might include going on training courses, obtaining secondments to another department, or asking for an interview with your boss or HR manager.

7. Remind yourself of your goals on a daily basis.

8. Go for the 'feel-good factor'. A goal may sound good, but it has to feel good, and that means it has to feel right for you.

9. Decide on a time-frame for achieving your goal.

10. Remember – it's your goal and you are responsible for achieving it.

When I ask clients to write down their work and career goals, they usually identify a desired state, such as being happy at work, being successful, being fulfilled, being challenged, developing and growing. The drawback is that they are not harnessing a goal. If you don't yet know what your goals are or what you want to do as a career, don't worry. In order to get your mind focused, begin by asking yourself the following questions:

- What sort of job would make me feel successful?

- What type of work would I find fulfilling?

- What areas do I like being challenged in – physically, mentally, creatively?

- What type of work would make me happy?

There is no universal scale for happiness, success and fulfilment; there is only personal interpretation. Your value list will help with this. A goal should always be relevant to the values you hold. There is nothing to be gained on a personal level when you set goals that aren't appropriate. Even if you like the idea of getting a promotion and the extra income, if you value the camaraderie at work more, promotion may not make you happy, if you end up being in charge of your former colleagues. So, when you are setting a goal, give some thought to how achieving it would change things on as many levels as you can.

Michael set himself a goal to become head of his research department. For several years he had worked as a researcher and although he enjoyed his work immensely, a passing comment from his wife about being overlooked for promotion got him thinking. Within six months he gained promotion. However, the nature of Michael's work changed and became almost completely administrative. He also had a lot more politics to deal with. While he was quite capable of doing the job, the reality was that he didn't enjoy it.

Michael was facing a major dilemma. Could he tell his boss that he had made a mistake putting himself forward for promotion? If he went back to his previous role would it look like demotion? But, it was his concern about what other people thought that caused the problem in the first place. Michael didn't actually seek promotion, but didn't like the idea that his wife thought he was being overlooked. I suggested that Michael discuss the situation with his wife. The outcome was that his wife wanted him to be happy, but she had been under the impression that a promotion was what he wanted and all he needed was a bit of a push.

Communicating your values helps to avoid misunderstandings. It was a relief for Michael to discover he had the support and respect of his wife, but he still had the difficult decision of telling his boss and dealing with work colleagues.

Michael decided to go back to his old job. It wasn't an easy decision. He worried how this decision looked to his colleagues and managers, and also that he 'ought' to feel more ambitious. But ultimately, Michael chose wisely. He is much happier doing what he loves and what he feels he is best at. As he is good at research, he has the respect and admiration of his co-workers. If a few of them think he can't 'hack it' higher up, he considers it a small price to pay for not dreading the prospect of work every morning.

It was a very different situation for John when he decided to pursue promotion.

John loved his work as an in-store window display trainer for a fashion outlet. He had lots of opportunities to demonstrate his creative skills and prepare examples of visually stunning displays. Promotion to regional trainer meant he would be working with experienced window dressers and fellow trainers who had all the practical expertise required. John's role was to focus on the mechanics of good teaching and training, also to keep all area trainers up to date with the sort of overall image the company wanted to project.

When John came to see me he was very clear about the changes his new role would involve. After years of using his practical skills he felt ready to develop new skills and apply his energy in a different way. His block was overcoming his fear of mastering new skills and moving away from doing something that now came so naturally. By coaching John to focus on his values he was motivated to overcome this fear because he valued new challenges and desired the respect his new position would give him from his peers. John was staying with his values and simply needed some guidance on using them as a strength to overcome fear.

When we are faced with these kinds of decisions we can't expect that there will always be an answer that is 100 per cent black or white, wrong or right. We may have to be prepared to sacrifice some smaller gains – in Michael's case, a bigger salary and status increase – for the bigger ones: true satisfaction and fulfilment.

Now you've set your personal values and your goals, you're ready to move on to the next key step – putting these in practice by finding the job that's right for you.

▪ Coaching Review

► Prioritise your values using the Formula.

► Let go of any limiting beliefs and values that are holding you back or no longer relate to you.

► When you are happy with your value list, write it in your journal for future reference.

► Make sure you are integrating your values into the workplace.

► Remember that reaching a compromise is not the same as being compromised.

► Identify why you work, listing reasons for having to work and choosing to.

► If work feels like a sacrifice or value conflict, you are either doing the wrong thing or doing it for the wrong reasons.

► Aim to achieve a balance between quantity and quality.

► Be specific about the goals you set for work and career.

► Goals should always be positive and about what you want to get out of life, not a life you want to get out of.

► Your goal must be relevant and appropriate to your values.

CHAPTER THREE

Finding the Right Job

THE RIGHT JOB IS the one that plays to your strengths, matches your talents and ambitions, and fits with your lifestyle. Identifying what 'the right job' means to you is essential if you're going to be happy and successful at work. Whether you're a first-time job seeker, ambitious for promotion and progress, already in the right job but with the wrong company (an important distinction), or searching for something completely different, you can discover what 'the right job' really means to you by using the Formula.

Any definition of 'the right job' is a very personal one. I can't give you a prescription, because there's no such thing – only jobs that are right or wrong *for you.* Rather like a jigsaw, you get to the big picture by looking at a lot of different parts: your values, goals, financial requirements, reasons for working, attitude, future plans and the relationship you have with work.

In Chapter 2 we began this process by identifying your values and why you work. Now it's time to expand on them and explore in more detail your work ethic and attitude towards work.

Personal values are your starting point and your compass – they give you guidance and direction. Along the way you may lose direction and take on a job that isn't what you thought it would be. That's fine – very few individuals get their career choice right first time. I certainly didn't. However, I've benefited from every single job I've ever done, ranging from working in a newsagents, nursing, having a market stall and being a waitress to working as a nanny, receptionist, beauty therapist, company director, business consultant, TV presenter, life coach and writer. I couldn't make that list up if I tried! My career path was so varied that it could have rendered me unemployable. But I didn't see it that way. I truthfully believed that it gave me a wide range of invaluable skills and experience. It's all too easy to think that the doors to success open for some people but not for other. Believing anything is possible and not sharing other people's limited expectations is what made the difference for me. Having a positive attitude about yourself and your work can make the same kind of difference for you.

▪ Changing the Way You Work

Some careers follow a far more structured path than the one I chose. But the old, traditional structures are becoming less rigid and well defined. In this new world of work, people are increasingly changing their careers completely, or choosing new and unconventional ways to find work. In the US, a recruitment company called Monster.com now lets people put details of their skills and experience on their website and then encourages employers to bid for them. It's just the beginning of a whole new way of looking at and engaging in work.

All this change can seem overwhelming and confusing, but there's also a lot of very positive side-effects to embrace and exploit. Andrew Wilkinson is the managing director of Monster.com in Europe, and he believes that many of the big changes in the way we work will benefit and empower employees. For a start, we're in a tight labour market – a condition that's forecast to remain with us for a long time. This means there just aren't enough good people to fill good jobs, so it's a sellers' market.

In this new world of work, according to Andrew Wilkinson, it's time to stop thinking about jobs or job titles at all. Instead, focus on what he calls your 'skill set'. Clearly defined job titles limit the areas you move into, whereas being able to define your skill set makes both you and the employer better aware of your true potential. Why be called an accountant if a skill set could reveal things like managerial, marketing and project development experience, and expertise in marketing and client liaison? Here are some more examples:

JOB TITLE	SKILL SET
Secretary	Administration, budgeting, organisation, project support, research
Salesperson	Project planning, communication, negotiation, marketing, client liaison
HR manager	Corporate strategy, communication, negotiation, administration, team development

Describing yourself in terms of your skills can open up whole new areas for you to move into, if you want to. That's a new world of opportunity, just from making a mental shift in the way you see and describe what you do. Which brings us to another key factor in finding the right job . . .

▪ It's a Question of Attitude

To find the right job you have to be in the right frame of mind. Feeling happy and successful is not a state that comes attached to a job description – it depends on your attitude, no matter what you do. We've probably all looked at someone else's job and thought 'If only I could do that I'd be happy', or imagined that certain careers are 'dream jobs' and problem-free. The truth is that work-related issues exist in all jobs. Gloomy message? I don't think so! Wouldn't it be sadder to think that feeling happy at work is only reserved for certain professions? It's just not the case.

> Gary has worked for 15 years in a DIY shop in London. He loves what he does and takes pride in his work, which is demonstrated by the level of his customer service. Gary is a mine of information and you can't help getting caught up in his enthusiasm and knowledge.

> Then there's Mary who works as a cleaner at a hospital. For the patients she makes as valuable a contribution as the medical staff. They love to see her cheerful face and hear her funny stories. For Mary, life and work are an adventure, and she can put a positive spin on anything.

The right attitude is essential – and immensely powerful. And the right attitude isn't something you're lucky enough to be born with. It's something everyone can work on, develop and improve. I've had clients who hoped that when they found the right job, their attitude would adjust accordingly, but that's rarely the case. Whatever job you have now, the best attitude to take is that at this moment it's the right job.

We all know that life is about relationships; you form relationships with people and with work. Happy and successful individuals have mastered the art of forming good relationships. They do this through practice and they take advantage of every opportunity they are given. Have you ever known a miserable person with the wrong attitude who suddenly transforms overnight into a happy-go-lucky individual?

That's why it is so important that whatever type of work you are doing at the moment you apply the right attitude, because if you aren't, it could be standing in the way of you finding the right job.

Jacky and Sara both started work on the same day for one of my corporate clients. Jacky was the office junior with few qualifications and no work experience. However, she had a very endearing way of asking for assistance. When asked to telephone a customer about an order, Jacky said she was worried that her telephone manner wasn't very good and what should she say so as not to put the customer off. It was delightful watching the whole office rally around and contributing the benefit of their experience. When she made the call, the rest of the staff were positively willing her on and quick to praise her efforts.

Sara had recently graduated from university with a first-class degree and was employed to organise and oversee European exhibitions. She spoke several languages, yet funnily enough seemed to have major problems communicating well. She started every sentence with a long sigh and was prone to rolling her eyes towards the ceiling. In the event that anyone made the oversight of offering to show her how to do something, she would briskly reply, 'I know, I know.' Unfortunately for Sara, she didn't know as much as she thought and was clearly oblivious to the impression she created.

Two weeks later I was discussing the new recruits' progress with Simon, one of the directors. He told me that it was unlikely they would be keeping Sara on after her probation period. Now it would have been difficult to fault Sara's work, although Simon took great delight in telling me she had mis-filed a document. Strangely enough, when Jacky had e-mailed a client saying Simon would be flying into 'Euston' airport instead of 'Houston', he found this hilarious. The bottom line was that he didn't like Sara's attitude

By all accounts Sara was very upset when the company didn't keep her on. This had been a job she really wanted, not that you would have known it from her attitude. Jacky, by contrast, was kept on and has now progressed well beyond office junior.

To put it simply, interpersonal skills are imperative to your future success. Regardless of the level at which you join a company, you're still the new kid on the block and everyone around you is waiting for you to make a good impression. Interpersonal skills are not about impressing people with your CV, how smart you are or how well you can perform a task. They are about how you impress people on a personal level, which comes down to whether or not they like you.

There's a simple rule I apply to having good interpersonal skills that will tell you all you need to know – make people feel good about themselves and they will find it much easier to like you. Use the following guidelines.

► Don't be afraid to ask for help.

► Demonstrate you are willing to learn by showing gratitude for any advice and assistance given.

► Show you are interested in other people by asking questions about them.

► Show respect for the experience, reputation and position of colleagues.

Even if you think you have found the right job it's important that your employer feels they have found the right employee. So begin as you mean to go on. Establish good working relationships in every job you do.

▪ Making Your Job Work for You

You may be dissatisfied with your current job, but changing it may be an option you don't want to take. Perhaps you are part of a long-term share saving scheme, or something similar that makes you want to stay where you are for a while longer. Or maybe you feel that your current company can offer good opportunities or other pluses elsewhere. So, how can you get the most from your existing job? Staying in the present and setting short-term goals will certainly help. Very often, when I ask clients to set work goals, they come up with a list that is unrelated to their current job, or they don't focus on the sort of job they are doing at that moment in time. I see lots of goals saying 'Change job', 'Get a promotion' or 'Change department'. There's nothing wrong with those aims, but to improve your current situation, positive goals can and should be set on a daily basis and they should be specifically related to what you do now. They should also be related to what you want from work. Use the Formula to help you do this.

Focus

Write down in your journal the reasons why you are dissatisfied with your existing situation. Be specific and relay the problem in the first person and define how the problem affects you, not anyone else. For example, 'I don't like the way my boss treats me' rather than 'My boss treats me badly.' Keep your goals focused on a positive action rather than just a negative reaction, so say, 'I need to increase my income' rather than 'I don't earn enough money'; 'My work is not as fulfilling as I'd like it to be' rather than 'My work is boring.' The way in which you describe a problem will indicate whether or not you are open to finding a solution. As a coach, I am very discerning about the clients I work with, because some people get stuck in a way of looking at their problems and won't try different options – and then they wonder why they keep hitting the same blocks. Focus on describing your problem in a way that opens you up to finding a solution.

Organise

Use your journal to list action-taking goals, so rather than just describe what you want, state what you are going to do about it. Begin each action goal with 'I am going to . . .'

- improve my relationship with my boss

- make my work more fulfilling

- increase my income

- do something positive to improve the atmosphere at work

- explore avenues for further training

- give more positive feedback to work colleagues

- prioritise my work better

- find ways to relax more and cut off at the end of the day.

The good thing about setting yourself action-taking goals is that they prompt you into finding a solution rather than staying focused on the problem.

> Mark, who worked for a firm of accountants, found the atmosphere very formal and he longed for a better sense of community. He took action in a rather unusual way. He loved yoga and found it a great way to relax, so he asked around the office if any of the staff would like to take part in yoga sessions in his office at lunchtime. Several of them did and this simple action not only created a better atmosphere, it also allowed the staff to share an experience that wasn't work related.

> Maria found herself struggling to keep her team of sales staff motivated to meet the Friday afternoon rush. By giving them positive feedback on their performance she found they were able to muster the enthusiasm and energy to race through the 6 o'clock deadline.

If you are dissatisfied at work you have to look for ways in which you can change things.

Review

This is a good time to review how you felt about previous jobs – were you more satisfied than now or less? Can you identify something that changed how you feel about your existing job? Have your needs changed? Has the company culture changed? Could the problem be related to internal changes, changes within you, rather than external ones, within the company? Are you trying to fit into company values instead of identifying your own values first? Are you getting caught up in office politics or other people's problems? Is this a new scenario or an old pattern repeating itself? Make a note of the results in your journal.

Motivate

Keep setting goals on a daily basis and note down your progress. You could begin with the goal: 'Today I am not going to complain about any aspect of my work' or 'I will make only positive statements today.' You'll be amazed how different you will feel at the end of the day. Sometimes a good moan with colleagues can help let off steam, but done frequently it will sap motivation. Goals that require you to be proactive rather than reactive are very good ones. Being reactive involves statements like 'I don't know what my boss expects from me.' A proactive goal would be 'Today I am going to ask my boss about the objectives of my job.' Here are some more examples:

- I will make at least one positive suggestion today about how a problem could be resolved.

- I will give positive feedback to a work colleague about their performance.

- I will ask for feedback on my own performance.

- I will spend time at the beginning of the day prioritising my work and making a list.

- Today I will focus on all the positive aspects of my job and write them down.

Utilise

This is where you focus on your strengths and skills – the arsenal that you will use to help you to overcome your problems and achieve your goals. So, what are your strengths? Everyone has them, though it can be hard to remember that when you're dealing with very tough or long-standing problems. Acknowledging that you have a problem is a strength. Having goals is always a strength. Taking responsibility for solving your problem is also a strength. Some others might include:

- I am hard working

- I am a fast learner

- I get on well with most people

- I have demonstrated that I am good at sales/admin/ideas/ teamwork.

Listing your strengths helps build your self-esteem and confidence that you have the ability to solve your problems. In other words, it pushes you into problem-solving mode, which is where you need to be. Excellent. And how can you use these strengths to change things? Well, acknowledging your own role in your problem helps you to change your attitude and your performance, for example. Being committed to resolving your problem may affect the way you communicate. It may also help you to be more assertive and motivate you to be clear about your boundaries.

Liberate

You may need to let go of some of your old ways of thinking and working in order to succeed. If you are prone to thinking 'There is nothing I can do to change things', then you will stay stuck. You need to stop thinking it isn't your responsibility, because it is. Simply highlighting problems to colleagues or employers rarely results in solutions. Every time you identify a problem, make sure you have come up with a few solutions.

Act

There is no point in setting goals if you don't act on them. You should be taking positive action every day to create the sort of working life you desire. Identifying what your real issues are will show you the sort of action you need to take.

▪ Knowing What You Want

Before you start to explore the different types of work and opportunities that are available you need to explore what you want from a job. The exercise below will help you do this.

EXERCISE

In Chapter 2 I asked you to select your reasons for working from a list of statements. As a follow-on exercise study the list below and put a tick next to any of the things you would expect from the right job. You can add to this list.

A pension plan	Professional qualifications
Medical insurance	Flexible working hours
Granting study leave	A sports or recreation club
Equal opportunities	A share saver scheme
Bonus package	Term-time contracts
Training	A confidential helpline service

Now study the following list, prepared by Ceridean Partners for their survey 'The Price of Success'. The list contains the main attractions to work. There is no specific order to this list, but you can re-work it or prepare your own list in order of priority for your journal. For a first-time job seeker, training and development may take priority over job security. If you have a mortgage and family to support, job security and money could feature higher on your list. You need to complete this section before you move on to the next exercise.

Professional challenge	Opportunities for a better work/life
Recognition of my contribution	balance

Job security

My team

Training and development
   opportunities

Money and benefit packages

Corporate culture

My boss

Flexible working arrangements

Market position/standing

▪ Right Job, Wrong Company

You love the job but you don't like the company. Simple solution: work for another company. Of course, it's not that easy. But you can start by acknowledging that you have found the *sort* of work you like doing, which immediately puts you ahead of the game. What you need to establish now is the problem with the company. You can use coaching methods to decide this.

Make lists in your journal under the following headings:

Goals These have to relate to your situation and any blocks you are experiencing. If your company offers no opportunities for promotion, your goal would be 'To get a promotion'. Perhaps you don't like the working culture. In this situation the goal would be 'To work in a friendly supportive culture'. If you are struggling to achieve a work/life balance the goal would be 'To achieve a work/life balance'. Starting to get the idea? Think about what the problem is and turn it into a goal.

Personal strengths Study the following list and then prepare your own list of personal strengths in a similar way.

- ▪ I am very loyal to my company

- ▪ I have excellent skills

- ▪ I am an excellent team worker

- ▪ I am very good at prioritising my work

- ▪ I am a popular member of staff

- ▪ I am extremely considerate to the needs of others

- ▪ I am good at delegating work and taking responsibility

- I never leave a job unfinished.

In Chapter 7 you will find out how to prepare a skills audit, listing all your skills, both technical and interpersonal.

Problems/blocks/challenges Now you can list any problems – relay them in the first person and word them in such a way that they allow you to find a solution. Better to say 'I need to find a means by which I can achieve promotion' rather than 'I can't find any opportunities for promotion.' This subtle change can switch the brain into problem-solving mode.

Development skills These are any skills you could acquire that would improve your situation. Again keep them specific to your problem. If getting your message across is difficult it may be your communication skills that need improving. Constant deadlines may be causing a problem and improving your ability to deal with stress would help. Being given unrealistic workloads may require you to be more assertive about your boundaries or to be less critical of your performance.

Achievements You need to chart your achievements constantly, as a positive reminder of your progress. Include everything you can think of: good time-keeping, successful projects, qualifications, skills, experience, reputation, remuneration, bonuses and references.

Once these steps are completed you can focus on finding a solution. Here are some useful coaching questions to help you through this process: What can I do to make these changes? How can I communicate my needs to the company? Is there a major value conflict or just a difference of opinion? Are my needs in line with company needs?

Getting the desired result does not have to mean moving to another company. The sensible thing is to explore all options available before making a decision. If you do decide it's time to make a move then the next thing you need is information, so keep reading.

▪ Dream On

What would your dream job be? Surprisingly, few people seem to be able to answer this question. Many seem to have lost their ability to dream, especially when it comes to work. If you are inclined to be dismissive about dreams, be careful. A common response is to say, 'Well I like to be realistic.' Good. But be careful that 'realistic' doesn't become 'pessimistic'. If you can't dream up your ideal job, what chance do you think you have of either finding it or creating the circumstances to get it? Many people make career choices for all the wrong reasons. A common reason is to pick something you are good at. It doesn't always follow that you will enjoy it.

In her inspiring book, *Working from the Heart*, Liz Simpson highlights that *capability* does not equal *suitability*. Job selection by both employee and employer is often based on capability and ignores suitability. You obviously know more about the sort of person you are than an employer ever could, so it's your responsibility to find the sort of work that suits the person you are. Again this comes back to values and having your own in place before you try to align them with a company. The world of work is full of very capable people who feel neither happy nor successful. Why? Because they are not doing what they want to be doing. The challenge I would like to set you for the next exercise is to dream up your ideal job.

EXERCISE

To get you started refer to your value list (from Chapter 2). Now relate each of those values to a work situation. Here are some examples of values, with hints on how to interpret them:

Family If family is a key value for you, give some thought to whether you would like to work for a small organisation or large one. You may be attracted to a family firm or company that treats you like one of the family.

Marriage Finding the right job is about forming a close relationship with the work you do and the people you work with.

Partners A good working relationship requires a good partnership. You may prefer to work in an environment where you are treated like an equal partner rather than an unequal subordinate.

Contribution You need to define exactly what you mean by 'contribution'. What is it you want to contribute? Do you see this as contributing your knowledge and expertise? Is it important to you that you contribute something that is socially and morally valuable to society, such as working in the leisure or catering industry, or working with homeless or disabled individuals?

Honesty Bearing in mind that companies are at times restricted to the information they can reveal to staff, how would you see honesty operating in the workplace? Make a list of the things that would satisfy your requirements.

For example:

► I would expect my employers to honour all the terms and conditions of my employment contract

► I would expect my employers to honour the promises made at my interview

► I would expect my employers to notify me of any changes to organisational goals.

Security What would make you feel secure in a job? A lengthy contract? A supportive boss? Good training?

Once you have completed the above exercise, you have to look for the sort of work that would allow you to incorporate your working values. It can be easy to think that only certain types of work meet your needs. But make sure you are not limiting your choice or only doing what others expect you to do. Considering a complete career change can be unnerving, but you have to see yourself in your dream job and believe it is an achievable goal. Now you can work through the Formula to find the right job.

▪ The Right Job Starts Here

Focus

Think about the type of work that you want to do and use the headings below to expand on this. Always talk in the first person and be as specific as possible. For example:

Type of work The type of work I would like to do would involve travel. It would be very people oriented and I could use my organisation skills and ability to communicate. There would be a very sociable element to the work with little time spent in an office or behind a desk.

Appealing jobs Working as a holiday rep, air steward, travel guide.

Type of company I want to work for a company that really values customer service and has a good reputation. The right atmosphere for me would be informal but efficient with a high level of support for the staff.

People I would be working with I want to work with people who are a similar age to me. They would be outgoing, fun, friendly and there would be a real team spirit.

This list provides a good starting point to get you focused.

Organise

Gather as much information as possible on the type of work you want, such as company brochures and application forms. You can select as many occupations as you like. Gathering information allows you to make informed choices. It helps to talk to people who are already doing the type of work you are interested in to see what it really involves.

Review

Begin by listing any past experiences you don't want to repeat. Perhaps you need to ask more questions at your next interview, or be more honest and state what it is you really want. This may be a good time to review your CV and update it. You can also review your skills. In order to land your dream job would you have to do further training? Gain more experience? Relocate? Change your attitude? Do some networking?

Motivate

Give yourself a deadline for achieving your goal. By contributing to it on a daily basis you will stay motivated. For example, if you are considering a completely new career you have to do something that will make your goal seem real and achievable. This can involve enrolling on a course, reading up on the subject, and attending relevant conferences and lectures.

Visualisation techniques are a great way to stay motivated, so imagine yourself actually doing your dream job. What would it feel like? What would the environment be like? And the people? If you are not familiar with visualisation techniques, I would suggest reading *The Elements of Visualisation* (see Further Reading), which is a good introductory book on this subject.

Utilise

Now it's time for a bit of networking. If this is a new idea to you and you find the prospect daunting, start with the people you know and feel comfortable with. Tell them what it is you are thinking of doing. You'll be amazed who they know in a similar or related field and what information or contacts they have. Networking should be a two-way process, so think about what help you can offer the person you network with. Trying to get something for nothing either backfires or leaves the person who assisted you reluctant to help in the future.

Liberate

The only person who can stop you finding the right job is you. So make sure you are not putting up obstacles or making excuses. What you believe is what you create. If you believe you won't find the right job then you will lack the initiative and motivation to create the circumstances that allow you to find it. However, belief creates the necessary opportunities. Stay focused on finding positive information and you will.

Act

Take at least one action today that will bring you closer to the job you desire. It may be a phone call to a company for more information, sending out your CV, role-playing interview techniques or making an appointment with the business adviser at the bank if you want to set up your own business. Taking action makes the goal more real and will give you the confidence to see it is achievable.

▪ Facing the Challenge

You have now used the Formula to establish your values, why you work, what you want from work and what your dream job would be. So now it's time to 'face' the challenge which is:

(Formula + Application + Change + Experience) = results

By applying the knowledge you have acquired from working through the exercises in this chapter you will have the *application.* This will create a *change* in your working life. This could be taking a more positive attitude to your existing job, applying for a new job, increasing hard skills or soft interpersonal skills, or pursuing your dream job. Perhaps you have discovered that your major requirements from work are already being satisfied and there are other areas that you need to change. The changes you make will create a new *experience.* Once you gain that experience you can record your *results.* Remember, the aim is that you achieve happiness and success at work. Every chapter in this book will assist you in getting closer to that goal.

If you haven't been prompted to make any changes so far, don't despair. There's a lot more to come and it may take more time to unlock your individual block. As long as you have identified your values and constantly refer to them, you'll be armed with the necessary back-up information to make the right decision. Taking action isn't easy. But happy and successful people don't pursue the easy option – they pursue the right one for them. Now that you've established just what the 'right' job means to you, and what elements that job needs to have to be compatible with your values, goals and needs, you're ready for the next step: discovering what kind of company culture you belong in. That's the subject of our next chapter and it will enable you to fit your 'right' job to the 'right' company, and put everything you have learnt so far into context.

▪ Coaching Review

▶ Re-evaluate your relationship to work. How you think about work affects how you feel about it.

▶ Do you have the right attitude? Even if you think you have found the right job an employer has to think they have found the right employee.

▶ If you want to make your existing job work for you, stay in the present and set short-term goals that are specific to the work you do. Take responsibility for helping to bring about and implement the changes you desire.

▶ Identify, in order of priority, what you want from work.

▶ If you like your job but not the company explore all options before making a move. What can you do to change things?

▶ Use the Formula to determine your dream job.

▶ Practise networking.

▶ Your present situation will change whether you like it or not. So decide how much time you want to spend being reactive to change and how much time being proactive.

▶ Is it time to take action?

▶ Are you ready to 'face' the challenge?

CHAPTER FOUR

Finding the Right Company Culture

COMPANY CULTURE MEANS, simply, 'the way things are done around here'. And the way things are done impacts directly on you and your values, needs, job security and satisfaction, recognition and reward, salary, level of training, motivation, behaviour, and your relationship to the company and people in it. Quite a list! In Chapter 3 we explored how you can discover what is the 'right' job for you, but that job has to be put in context. The culture of a company is the context. There's no point in having the 'right' job if it's in the 'wrong' place, and you end up feeling alienated by the values, objectives, management style or atmosphere of the organisation. And that's why understanding company culture and finding the right one for you is an essential part of the Formula, and of your happiness and success at work.

In this chapter we will be exploring what contributes to company culture, finding out how to reveal the real culture of an organisation and applying the Formula to find out the best working culture for you. You can also use the Formula to influence the culture of the organisation you work for now.

▪ How Important Are You?

There are many companies that genuinely care about their staff. However, considering that 'lack of recognition' is one of the major reasons for discontent at work, clearly there are also plenty of companies that don't.

Companies are often quick to say, 'People are our most important asset', which is good to hear, even if it is stating the obvious. People have always been the most important asset and always will be! Technology may have created virtual companies, where trading takes place on line, but that doesn't – and won't – take people out of the picture.

Any business you care to identify is about trading. A business trades goods, services, information and skills, but it also trades in relationships. Even if you order products over the Internet your needs still have to be met on a human level. Somebody has to deliver it, for a start. Then you may have other requirements, such as being made to feel like a valued customer, getting good and accurate information and after-sales service.

I read a rather disconcerting quote from a chairman of a major company who reportedly said, 'Quality of life should follow economic growth.' That statement, unfortunately, sums up what is still the real attitude of a lot of companies, namely: profit comes before people. When that's the case, this message becomes ingrained into the culture of a company. If you're choosing where to work, it's important for you to look beyond the mission statements, glossy PR brochures and customer services leaflets of an organisation, because preaching a message is not the same as practising it. This chapter will show you how to do just that. The best working culture for you is one that meets your expectations and is in line with your values.

▪ Effects of Company Culture

Like me you have probably been on the receiving end of poor customer service. When my new dishwasher flooded my kitchen floor and I called the company in question, they bounced me around from one department to the next. Although I found the situation frustrating, the staff working there really had my sympathy. When you're on the receiving end of bad customer service it can be easy to think the staff have an attitude problem, but if it's an attitude reflected throughout the organisation, the blame lies with the company. In order for you to perform well at work an employer has to create an environment that allows you to. If you worked in a call centre handling customer complaints, but the company policy was to get customers off the phone as quickly as possible, you would find it very difficult to do your job well.

Culture is intangible, a powerful and often unspoken code. Without realising it you can start to adopt the behaviour and culture of a company. It starts on the simplest levels. Imagine your first day in a new job. On your way to the coffee machine you ask if any of your colleagues would like one. As the day goes on you notice staff going to and from the machine, but they only get themselves a coffee. A few days later you are doing the same thing without really noticing. See what I mean about the simplest things? There are of course positive aspects of company culture you can adopt. For instance, if giving positive feedback is the norm this could be a good habit you soon slip into.

Rob worked in senior management for a large insurance firm. He contacted me six months into his new job. Rob liked the work, but he found it very difficult to adapt to the company culture. His previous employers were very informal, with a teamwork approach. In contrast the insurance firm was formal and hierarchical.

I met up with Rob at his office. As I was a few minutes early I chatted with his secretary. She was wearing a sparkling ring, which I admired. With a beaming face she told me she had got engaged the previous week. Her husband had left her ten years ago to bring up two children. Just when she had given up on the idea of having a relationship a wonderful man came into her life.

In my meeting with Rob I listened for ten minutes to him telling me how unfriendly and formal the people were at his company. How his immediate boss probably had no idea if he was married, had children, what his interests were. I sympathised, but decided to spend a few minutes getting Rob to focus on his own behaviour and attitude.

To begin with I asked questions about his secretary. Was she married? He didn't know. Did she have any children? He didn't know. What were her interests? He didn't know. Had she only recently started working for him? No, she had worked for him since he joined the company six months ago. I didn't have to ask anything else about his secretary – Rob got the point of my questions.

Next we discussed values. Position and status were very important to him. Although Rob didn't like the indifferent attitude of his bosses, he was honest about liking the kudos of his own position and the hierarchy that existed. The friendly team spirit of his previous job made him feel recognised by his boss, but he had hankered after prestige and recognition of his rank by colleagues. By exploring his personal values and the difference between his previous power-sharing work culture and his current power-controlling position, Rob decided that, overall, this culture was actually one that suited him and satisfied his major values. Now that Rob was also aware of his own behaviour he decided to set himself a goal to create a friendlier atmosphere in his own department.

When I spoke to Rob the following week he was delighted with the results of his new approach. Not only was he having more fun at work, but also his boss had commended him for the sudden productivity increase in the department. It's amazing what a shift in perspective can do. By changing his own attitude and the way he treated people Rob improved the immediate working culture, got the recognition of his boss and maintained the kudos he desired.

This story is very significant. It highlights the importance of being honest with yourself, as Rob was, and it shows how you can adopt a company culture, even when you don't like some aspects of it. Coaching is not about making a judgement about 'right' or 'wrong' values or culture. You have to establish what's right for you and recognise that you can satisfy your values without adopting inappropriate behaviour. If you want the people below you to look up to you, does that mean you look down on them? Of course not. Status can be achieved through respect for what you do, not just who you are in the pecking order.

▪ The Company Culture Checklist

In hindsight we often know the questions we should have asked at an interview, or the things we should have picked up on about a company's culture. Much of what you are told at interview is open to interpretation and in order to uncover the real culture you have to understand what certain statements mean. For example, a company may describe itself as being 'very informal'. This has been used to mean any of the following:

- a messy and chaotic workplace

- flexible working hours

- vague job description

- a power-sharing work culture

- no secure job contracts

- jeans and T-shirt are OK

- there is a team spirit and relaxed division of ranks

- senior management have very plush offices, while the rest of the staff work in noisy, open-plan ones

- all staff comments and complaints are treated with equal status and investigated

- there is no procedure for communicating your needs and grievances

- a day off can be booked at short notice

- if you want time off, don't expect to be paid

- as long as the job is done it's OK to arrive late or leave early

- there will be regular unpaid overtime.

As you can see, you really need to know how statements are converted into action, because that determines the working culture.

I have devised a checklist for you to use to help you define a company's culture:

1. Place

2. Atmosphere

3. Values

4. Reputation/story

5. Behaviour

This list has proved invaluable for my clients when they have either been considering working for a particular company or want to understand the real culture of their existing workplace. Culture is not one-dimensional; there are numerous facets that contribute to and influence it. They don't all have to be in place or to your liking for you to find the right culture for you. This checklist can help you determine what to look for, if there are some things you can reach a compromise on and what matters to you most. It forms the basis for the exercise at the end of this chapter.

Below are some pointers to get your thoughts moving in the right direction.

1. Place

This is the place of work. What do the premises look like? Some companies spend vast amounts of money on a plush reception area, yet fail to follow through in other areas. A bank I visited recently had expanded its reception area. It looked very impressive to customers, but the problem was that the staff were pushed to the back of the building and worked in cramped conditions. Result: miserable staff.

Some workplaces won't be pristine and luxurious. But they can still be comfortable and functional. When a company cares about the well-being of its staff they are provided with a well thought out workplace. Are you working in a well-organised place or falling over mess? Are you breathing fresh air or wheezing through the air-conditioning system? What's displayed on the walls and noticeboards also indicates culture. It could be formal notices and messages, staff incentives, humorous captions, posters that depict values like a charity appeal or political slogans.

Spend a few minutes thinking about what your workplace is like, how you would like it to be or the sort of place you would like to work in. If you work from home, this category is still relevant because you can create your own workspace.

2. Atmosphere

Think about your favourite restaurant. Chances are the ambience is just as important as the food. Likewise, when it comes to the workplace, the atmosphere should reflect what goes on there. Even within the same company there can be a different mood throughout the building. The accounts department could feel formal compared to the sales department, for example.

To get it right for you, first think about what your job involves, and then think about the kind of atmosphere that would be appropriate for it. Certain professions, like the legal profession or a health and safety department, follow very methodical procedures. So you wouldn't expect an atmosphere of 'anything goes'. An appropriate atmosphere for your job would be more formal and structured. If your work requires you to be creative and forward thinking you may perform best in an environment that is not regulated by rituals and procedures. Here, the appropriate atmosphere might be highly informal and unstructured.

Like culture, atmosphere is an unspoken code of what's acceptable. Ask yourself: Is it acceptable to have fun here, try something different, use my initiative, put forward suggestions, give feedback, expect to be valued, have clearly defined procedures?

Generally speaking, problems don't arise when a company creates an atmosphere that is appropriate to the nature of the work carried out there. Obviously there will be those who find it's not right for them – a case of a mismatch of individual needs and company needs. That's why it's crucial that you take responsibility for the selection process: it's up to you to assess the suitability of a company while the company is assessing yours.

3. Values

Remember that to get the most from your job you have to be working in line with your values and goals. Companies also have values and goals. They want things that range from staff productivity, discipline and loyalty, to ideas, creativity, forward thinking and a commitment to organisational goals. In order to get these they have to meet your expectations about your working life, what you want from it and what you value. If your expectations are not met you may still work hard, be loyal and even productive, but you will find it very difficult to be committed to your company's values, visions and goals.

Let's say a company has a major goal to increase profit by upping productivity 40 per cent. If you were made to feel valued by better job security, an increase in salary and a profit-sharing scheme it would be a lot easier to share that goal. But if it meant longer hours, harder work, added pressure and no financial incentive you would be far less inclined to share that goal. So think about how your company plans to achieve its goals and objectives, as this is where it will demonstrate its values. Goals are often influenced by commercial objectives, but many companies demonstrate their commitment to people-centred values at the same time.

Companies don't always practise the attractive values they preach, so you must look for evidence. Refer back to your own value list (from Chapter 2) and think about how a company could demonstrate similar values. If you value recognition, what would make you feel appreciated? If you need a work/life balance, how could they help you achieve this? The two crucial questions are 'Am I clear about this company's values and organisational goals?' and 'Can I make a commitment to them?' Unless you can, your values will be compromised.

4. Reputation/story

Suzanne O'Leary is a director at PR firm Shandwick Miller. Before finalising her decision to work there she wisely checked out their reputation. PR companies work very closely with the press and media, so who better to ask than journalists? The feedback she received was very positive and Suzanne was able to determine that her objectives about the sort of company she wanted to work for would be met. So, if you want to check the reputation of a company talk to people who deal with them such as their suppliers and customers or, if possible, employees.

It's not just a case of finding a company with a good reputation; you have to find one that fits your values. An advertising agency with a reputation for being highly creative sounds appropriate, but imagine if an accountancy firm had the same reputation. Do you want to work for a company that has a reputation for being the market leader? Or what about being innovative, competitive, financially sound, dynamic, formal, informal, socially conscious, service orientated?

When a company is too new to have built up a reputation, look for the story. Every company has one, even on the first day of business. The story of a company will be told to you at an interview, by staff working there and often by clients and customers. It won't always align with its reputation, but it is one of the best indications of culture. All you have to do is listen intently and you'll get the message.

At any interview you will receive a huge amount of information, even if you are told very little. That may sound like a contradiction, but when a company withholds information you already know they are not good at information sharing, they aren't going to treat you like an equal, they don't value communication and their recruitment procedure leaves a lot to be desired. So you are already starting to get the story.

Most companies provide a pretty complete story. You can expect to be told about their history, what makes them different, what their aims and objectives are, how influenced they are by the market place, and what their mission and values are. Look for any recurring themes, because that's the real story. When I visited a new therapy treatment centre in London the one thing I kept hearing was that it was the largest of its kind. This would have seemed relevant for a bank or supermarket. Being the largest could indicate success or customer choice. But I expected to hear stories about the quality of the therapists, the superb treatments on offer, customer satisfaction. This is an example not only of a company getting it wrong, but also of how the story revealed the company's mistakes by what it chose to relay as being significant.

Some companies build up mythical stories. They may not be strictly true, but they serve as symbolic examples of how things are done. Like the one about the owner of a car showroom who used to visit the premises in the evening, put on a white glove and check the car bonnets for dust. This tale was relayed to all new recruits. Why? Because it was a funny yet powerful way to get the message across that the company valued immaculate showrooms. A story can be a much more effective way to get a message across than an instruction, and it can also enforce what is expected and acceptable.

Positive stories about staff being rewarded for their efforts through pay rises or bonuses would motivate you. Negative stories about staff being sacked or reprimanded as a means to enforce discipline or get you to toe the line would demotivate you. So pay attention to the stories you are hearing.

5. Behaviour

This is probably the most immediately revealing aspect of culture. Although we all have individual behaviour patterns, they tend to merge with the group culture at work. That's OK when you are happy and in the right environment, but when you aren't the traits you develop will be less desirable.

Some professions are associated with certain character traits. You wouldn't be surprised to find a sales person with the gift of the gab or an IT expert who spoke in technical shorthand. Job titles often dictate the way we behave. With the loss of clearly defined job titles in many sectors the way things were done has changed. This not only affects behaviour – it can cause confusion.

> Recently I was trying to get some information from a company and was put through to Julie. Not sure if she would be able to help me I asked her position and was informed she was a team leader. 'What's that?', I enquired. 'Someone who leads a team', was the reply. That kind of behaviour could easily be deemed unhelpful and incompetent. Julie's behaviour does not necessarily reflect her ability. It could reflect the culture of an organisation that hasn't installed effective procedures and training. Without these in place your ability to perform well will be severely hampered, and this can affect your attitude and behaviour. If the company doesn't care, why should you?

Many companies complain that they can't find good staff. I don't buy that. Yes there are individuals in the workplace with a bad attitude. But groups of individuals in a workplace behave in a way that is in line with the organisation's values. The minute you walk into any reception area you get an indication of what's to come. Are you going to be made to feel welcome? Or are you going to be left standing while staff talk among themselves?

I've seen excellent employees deteriorate rapidly by being in the wrong culture, so I can't emphasise enough the importance of finding a culture that will nurture your potential.

▪ Your Role in a Changing Culture

You probably have no trouble adapting to change when you are in control of it and you can do it at your own pace. Resistance comes from what is perceived as imposed change. But often we fail to see how we act as a catalyst to change. Knowing the part you play in the process of change is key to feeling comfortable and better equipped to adapt to the unexpected.

The workplace is constantly changing. Takeovers, mergers, the introduction of newer and newer technology – change is the very lifeblood of business, and nothing can remain static or it will just wither and die. We often find this unsettling, but you may have overlooked the fact that, as a nation of obsessive consumers, the workplace has to constantly update to meet *our* demands. Getting the latest gadget, fastest service and access to all kinds of information has become an ingrained part of our culture. So it's not simply a case of the multinationals, stakeholders and government dictating the future and how it should be. We, the consumers, are part of the driving force. When you are in the middle of that change it can be difficult to see the bigger picture, how you fit into it and the input you have in creating it.

Knowing what's coming next is reassuring. Few people go through life always expecting the unexpected. However, in order to successfully deal with change you may need to rethink how you expect or predict the future to be. There is a technique I use in coaching called 'changing the running order', that will help you do this. The brain is often racing ahead to predict what comes next, how a sequence of events will go. Even when the running order is provided as it is, for example, with a film or TV programme, chances are you are still predicting how the characters will react, what comes next and if it will be a happy ending. These predictions are based on how you see the world. When you encounter a problem there is interference to your running order. Now, what looks like a problem to one individual will not be perceived as a problem to another. Why? Because they have a different running order. If you have a very restricted running order, it makes sense that you will experience more interference and therefore more problems. And fear of change is a major contributor to a restricted running order.

You may feel that the more changes you encounter in life the more problems you will face. But that's not the case when you are prepared to have lots of running orders. All you have to do is increase the number of predictions you make. Put simply this means considering several outcomes for a situation rather than limiting yourself to just one. Change may still pose some problems, but you will have a lot more flexibility dealing with it when you have a few contingency plans. Just because there are changes taking place at work doesn't mean you can't pursue your goals; it may simply be a case of using a different route to get there. A restructuring programme could delay your planned promotion – so you resist it. But you may not have considered the positive advantages. It could be that the restructuring programme brings about a better way of working and provides more opportunities than were previously available to you. Change will always cause you a problem when you predict a negative outcome. Change, not stability, is now the norm – it's worth remembering that it is often for the better.

Continually setting new goals is also a great way to deal with change because new goals stop you becoming stagnant and complacent. To achieve a new goal you can't stay where you are; you have to face new challenges, learn new skills and have new experiences.

▪ Finding the Right Working Culture for You

In the next exercise you will work through the Formula to find the right working culture for you. Whether you are job hunting or in an existing workplace you can do this exercise.

Focus

Go through your company culture checklist headings (place, atmosphere, values, reputation/story, behaviour). From your list you need to identify what is important to you. List the good things, for example 'I work in comfortable surroundings, my office has natural light and there is plenty of working space.' If you are dissatisfied with any area, don't list the problems – list your ideals. Rather than say, 'My workspace is cluttered and cramped', say, 'I want to work in a clutter-free office with lots of space.' Remember to identify what you want, not highlight the problem.

Organise

Write down the three headings below to organise your thoughts and feelings. I have deliberately used some examples of what may not work for you, but does for an employer. For your own list, see if there are any parts of your working culture that you don't like, but which may be a necessary part of the organisation. So, if you don't like constant deadlines, is it possible that they have to be in place to allow your company to survive in a competitive market place? This list will help you to see what areas you can compromise on and are willing to accept without feeling too stressed, resentful or unhappy. You can adapt this list if you are looking for a job and just use the first two headings, covering your likes and dislikes.

WHAT WORKS FOR ME	WHAT DOESN'T WORK	WHAT WORKS FOR THE COMPANY
The friendly team		The friendly team
The level of challenge		How I meet this
	The constant deadlines	My output
The company's professional reputation		Professional reputation
Updating skills		Staying ahead
	Work intensification	Increased output

Both employer and employee have to compromise on certain aspects. Only you know your own bottom line about working conditions.

Review

Review the times at work when you feel happiest. Make a list in your journal of what creates those circumstances. Is it being absorbed in a project, receiving praise, being part of the team, the social interaction, learning a new skill, teaching others skills or feeling valued for the job you do? From the company culture checklist, refer to as many sections as you can. Was the *place* you were working in particularly pleasant? Was there a good *atmosphere*? Were your *values* being satisfied? Were there positive *stories* circulating and did your *behaviour* reflect how you felt?

If you haven't worked before you can still review what makes you feel happy, productive, creative and motivated. Do you perform well in team activities or do you prefer completing projects on your own? Do you like lots of direction and supervision or are you a self-starter?

Motivate

Recreating the circumstances at work that make you happy will motivate you. To begin with concentrate on recreating the mood; remember how you felt at the time. What would it take for you to feel like that again? Do you think it is possible to feel like that regularly at work? If not, is it time to change job or company?

Utilise

Use your strengths. Are you getting the most from work by reminding yourself about all the positive aspects? Use your journal to list them. You may have formed strong bonds with colleagues, improved your financial position, gained valuable skills and experience, successfully completed projects or built up a great reputation. Knowing your strengths allows you to see that you may already be achieving many of the things you want from work and therefore the culture may be satisfying your needs on more levels than you realised.

Liberate

Are there any beliefs that are holding you back, like thinking you'll never find the right culture, or there is nothing you can do to improve it? You can affect the culture because it is the attitude and behaviour of individuals that help to create it. Culture is not set in stone; it is constantly evolving. In the past the people at the top often dictated the culture of an organisation, but things have changed. Individuals are demanding a better work/life balance, and they are not prepared to meet the demands of a workplace that is not prepared to meet *their* demands.

Act

Now you know the sort of company culture that suits you best, there are lots of thing you can do to take action. You can improve your immediate working environment by changing your own behaviour and attitude as Rob (who we met at the beginning of this chapter) did. If you are job-hunting you can take responsibility for asking the right questions like, 'What are the objectives of this company?' 'What is the company's vision for the future?' and making observations about the company culture.

Follow this through by looking for evidence. Being told at an interview that a company always listens to its staff and is committed to taking care of their needs is reassuring, but only when they can support this. When this is genuinely the case a company should be happy to demonstrate just how it does this, be it regular staff meetings, suggestion boxes, flexible working hours etc.

Perhaps your action could be to discuss an aspect of culture that is causing you a problem. Employers may not be aware of how you feel. They may have set up a system that was intended to provide clear guidelines about how you work and it could be that you find this rigid structure limiting. Don't be afraid to put your case forward, especially when you are prepared to offer an alternative that benefits both sides. If starting work later in the day and finishing later would suit you, consider why this might appeal to your employer. Would it allow you to take a later lunch and therefore provide cover during a busy period, for example?

Culture is certainly an intricate web, but you can avoid getting caught up in the wrong one for you, when you take responsibility for finding the right working culture and, where necessary, moving on from the wrong one. Remember, not only are you affected by the culture of an organisation, you also play a role in creating and contributing to it, so keep this in mind when you conclude this chapter, which means you have to 'face' the challenge:

(**F**ormula + **A**pplication + **C**hange + **E**xperience) = **results**

▪ Coaching Review

► 'The way things are done around here' is the simplest way to sum up company culture.

► Finding the right culture is as important as finding the right job.

► Be honest about what you value the most from work, remembering that it is possible to satisfy your major values and make some compromises along the way.

► People are the most important asset to any organisation. Make sure you pick a company that reflects this in its culture.

► If there are aspects of a company culture you don't like, make sure you are not repeating them in your own behaviour and attitude.

► Use the company culture checklist – place, atmosphere, values, reputation/story, behaviour.

► Having a flexible running order and predicting several outcomes helps you deal with change.

► You are part of a company's culture and you have the power to influence it.

► Don't be afraid to let a company know how you feel. Change can only take place when individuals are prepared to take action.

► If you are looking for a job, not only do you need to ask questions that relate to culture, you also have to look for evidence.

CHAPTER FIVE

Have You Got What it Takes to Be In Charge?

D o you want to be a leader? Is it your ambition to be in charge where you work, or to be your own boss, working for yourself or running your own company? If it is, then this chapter is for you. I firmly believe that we can all achieve great things – often more than we ever thought we could – with the right attitude and application. But leadership isn't for everyone.

Some people love the idea of the status and perks that come with being in charge, but haven't thought through the implications of the long hours, pressure and responsibility it takes to get there. And some people are prepared to work as hard and as long as they need to, but just haven't got the right skills. Being in charge needs a wide range of skills and abilities – it's no good just depending on your natural talents and hoping they will compensate for any skill gaps or inadequacies. If you really want to be a leader, this chapter can help you avoid the major pitfalls and achieve your goal. It is a challenging chapter – but if you've got what it takes, you'll be up for the challenge.

▪ What Do You Expect?

Not all promotions involve additional responsibility or even a change to your job. For example, in some banks, you may be placed on a higher grade and receive a higher salary because you have more qualifications or have passed an exam.

But most promotions do bring extra responsibility and increased workloads. There can be changes to your work objectives and the way in which your performance is measured. If you worked as a sales rep, for example, your objectives could be to meet monthly targets and this would be how your performance was measured. But if you got promoted to area sales manager your objectives could change to motivating a sales team and ensuring they *all* met their monthly targets, and you would be measured on their performance as well as your own. This may seem obvious, but you would be surprised at the number of people who don't give enough thought to what promotion means and how it will affect them.

One complaint I hear regularly from bosses is that many staff request a promotion for doing the job they are employed to do.

Fiona, a fairly new recruit to a company, requested a promotion because she had been involved in a presentation that secured a new client for the company. Now, her team regularly secured a client – that's what they were supposed to do – and there was no evidence that Fiona had met any objectives beyond those expected. A promotion would have meant her meeting much higher requirements in terms of both performance and responsibility, such as demonstrating strong interpersonal skills or a sound understanding of meeting company policy and objectives.

Her boss asked her to identify what she had done beyond what was normally expected, and what she thought would be required of her if she were given a promotion. It turned out that Fiona was unclear about what was meant by 'the basic requirements' of her job, or what would be deemed as exceeding them. She was also unsure about what level of experience she should have to be in line for a promotion. What she really needed were clearer guidelines, and examples of how she could improve her performance without taking on tasks or responsibilities that she didn't yet have the experience to deal with.

Fiona's case illustrates an important point: doing your current job well doesn't make you an automatic candidate for promotion. Within every organisation there are always staff who are good at their job, but they are not all in line for promotion. Why? Because a company seeks a particular and specific type of leader, one that is not only competent at their job, but whose skills and attitude also reflect that organisation's particular culture and objectives.

Winning promotion often means that we first need to gain more experience so we can understand what our new roles and responsibilities really involve. How you go about getting the right experience to achieve results varies from one organisation to another. In some organisations you may be thrown in at the deep end and left to learn as you go, whereas other organisations will have clear guidelines, procedures and policies to follow. There can also be training that covers things like people management, team building and staff motivation.

Learning as you go is a tough challenge, and you'll need to take into account the sort of company you work for before pursuing promotion. If there are no set guidelines to follow, you'll have to learn in other ways what is expected from you, what results are the most valued, and how to expand your responsibilities and influence. Some individuals love to learn on their feet, even when this means there is the added risk of making mistakes. Others prefer a more structured route with less risk and a gradual transition into a new role. You will need to decide which you are.

▪ Are You the Right Candidate for Promotion?

As discussed in Chapter 4, company culture dictates how things are done. To be the right candidate for promotion you have to satisfy the needs of the company as well as your own needs. Being in charge is very different from one organisation to another.

In some organisations results are achieved by following clearly defined policies and procedures. These organisations produce *Structural Leaders*. The public sector, for example, which often needs to demonstrate probity (defined as accountability, honesty and integrity), has a clear set of guidelines in terms of how decisions are made and how things are done. While some individuals prefer to have more personal decision-making freedom, others would see an advantage in the fact that they are not held personally accountable for a decision when they are following company procedure. When problems arise we tend to blame the 'system' rather than an individual leader.

Other companies produce what I call *Visionary Leaders* such as Anita Roddick and James Dyson. These are leaders who have more decision-making freedom. How things are done in these companies is not primarily achieved through procedures and systems, but through a set of deeply embedded values and cultures. While there is a much greater decision-making freedom, you may also be asked to demonstrate a higher level of personal responsibility. Again, any problems are blamed on the strongest visionary leaders rather than the company as a whole.

There are also many organisations that will produce leaders who fall between the two types. There will be a certain amount of procedures and policies to follow, and flexibility for decision-making freedom in other areas. It's important to understand the kind of company you work for, and the kind that best suits your own style and leadership potential.

You could find yourself in a situation where you don't like the sort of management your company produces. Leaving may not be an option, so whether or not you can progress to promotion comes back to your values. Let's say you value good communication and management is not good at listening to staff. It is possible to meet company criteria, which could be for strong dictatorial managers, and still meet your own values by maintaining good communication and interpersonal skills like listening, giving positive feedback and clear direction.

▪ Getting a Promotion

Why do you want a promotion? You may well deserve one, but unless you want it for the right reasons and are aware of what it will involve, it won't make you happy. So, before I talk about the sort of skills you'll need, make a list in your journal using the following heading, 'Why I want a promotion':

► For the extra income

► For the kudos

► I want to be challenged

► It will give me better job security

► I value leadership

► It will help me achieve my goals

► To improve my self-esteem

► I believe I can do the job well

► I need to feel I've achieved something

► I believe my hard work should be rewarded

► It would make me feel recognised

► It would give me additional skills

► I'm good at taking responsibility

► People keep telling me I should go for it

► I don't like constantly being told what to do and having other people dictate my working day

► I like being in a position that allows me to make decisions

► To gain the respect of colleagues

► To nurture and develop others.

You may have other reasons why you want promotion. The list is simply there to get you thinking about your own motivation, and to help get your priorities in place so that you are clear why you are pursuing this goal. You also need to be sure that your goals are in line with your values. Making the Formula work for you means not only knowing what your values are but also living by them.

▪ Overlooked for Promotion?

If your problem is that you are constantly overlooked for promotion, here are some guidelines to help you overcome this.

1. Remember: being good at your job doesn't automatically mean promotion. Many employers want you to exceed the objectives and expectations of your job.

2. Job descriptions are not always specific and can also expand. You should clarify – ideally in advance – exactly what your objectives are. If, for example, they are to increase productivity or sales, try to get your boss to specify by how much. If your target is a 20 per cent increase, then you know what you have to do to exceed this. If this is not clarified you may both have very different ideas of what is expected of you.

3. Always know on what basis your performance is measured. You will obviously be assessed on many levels, but you need to know what areas significantly influence you getting a promotion. For example, you may meet sales targets as well as a colleague, but your boss could be looking for the individual who creates the best team spirit or works best under pressure.

4. Ask for feedback. It demonstrates a commitment to doing your job well, and there's no point assuming you're performing brilliantly if others don't agree. Be prepared for negative feedback and don't be defensive. You may not agree with it, but we often base performance on our own standards, which won't necessarily match those of an employer.

5. Don't be afraid to discuss areas you are not strong in. Work situations are often competitive and you may believe that if you expose a weakness it will put you at a disadvantage. But if you are being overlooked for promotion, chances are your boss has already noticed it. By being proactive, you can turn a weakness into a strength.

Jason worked in sales. He came to see me because in the past year he had been on the shortlist for promotion from an area sales rep to senior sales co-ordinator twice, and missed out on both occasions. He couldn't understand why, because he had the highest sales figures. When Jason asked why he didn't get the job the first time round he was told that the candidate that did was simply the best applicant. Jason could have asked in which areas the other candidate was stronger. Instead, he mentally rejected that judgement and told himself that something underhand had gone on.

When it happened a second time Jason was fuming and his ego was too dented to even request feedback.

I asked Jason to list his strengths and weaknesses. I noticed that paperwork and administration were listed as a weakness. When I asked Jason about this he was initially defensive, 'The amount of paperwork is ridiculous. I worked most of last weekend filling in my expense forms and writing up my monthly sales report and all my boss did was complain that it was late even though I had the best sales figures this month.' I then asked Jason to put himself in his boss's position, because if he gained promotion this is exactly where he would be.

We discussed the objectives and responsibilities he would have, which included submitting all the sales reps' reports and expenses at the end of the month. I gave Jason a few minutes to let this sink in, then asked him what could be holding him back from promotion. 'Well I'm not very good at paperwork, but I'm great at sales and I really know how to motivate a team.' Time for a few tough coaching questions. I asked Jason if he thought his strengths were enough to compensate for his weakness and get him a promotion. 'Yes,' he replied. Did anyone else agree with him? He flinched at this question and said, 'It looks as if they don't.'

Now Jason had to find a solution, which would involve him improving his administration skills. I encouraged him to consider ways of involving his boss and colleagues in the solution. Finally Jason came up with the idea of calling a meeting to see if there was any alternative system that would reduce the level of paperwork for everyone, and therefore increase the efficiency of sales.

The meeting was a great success. Although sales is usually a highly competitive area, there were advantages for all the team in sharing ideas and techniques that would boost their sales and therefore their commission. Jason also learnt that contrary to what he believed he actually had no problem with administration when he saw it as useful instead of unnecessary. When the next promotion came up, he got it.

A willingness to acknowledge weaknesses and to work to overcome them are the sort of attributes that make a good leader. Promotion brings with it many new challenges and your attitude has to reflect that you have the ability to overcome them.

▪ Essential Skills

The skills I'm about to discuss are equally important for getting a promotion, becoming self-employed or running your own business. They are the essentials, but it's an ever-evolving list. The aim is to constantly increase and improve on the skills you have. That way you show a commitment to doing the best possible job.

Self-discipline

At work, other people often dictate what you do and when you do it. But that changes with promotion, self-employment and running a business. You can suddenly find yourself responsible for planning and prioritising your own time and other people's. To assess how good your self-discipline is, consider areas that are not work related. For example, do you go to the gym regularly? Can you resist having one drink too many? Can you keep your finances in order? Do you leave lots of tasks at home unfinished? Do you over-commit to doing things on your days off? In short, can you manage your time effectively and constructively, because that's the basis of self-discipline?

Communication

This is an essential life skill for everyone and one you really need to develop if you want to progress and succeed at work. A good tip is to get a clear picture in your head of what it is you want. One of the most frustrating situations for staff is to have someone in charge who is vague and gives confusing instructions. Bosses often talk about wanting to see staff using their initiative, but this can be very difficult for them to do without clearly expressed guidelines. You will need to focus on the results you want to achieve and take responsibility for communicating them.

Nurturing

Your ability to nurture and help others develop their potential is a real value system checkpoint. Unless you are prepared to respect other people, recognise their ability without feeling threatened by it and allow them to fulfil their real potential then my advice is: don't pass go until you have mastered this skill. The expectations of the workforce have changed, in my opinion for the better. We are no longer prepared to tolerate or co-operate with selfish, incompetent and insensitive bosses.

I've already emphasised the importance of communicating what you want. To succeed as a nurturing leader means being clear about the results you want to achieve without feeling the need to dictate the *process,* which is how staff do their jobs. You can establish the right environment by implementing good training, role models and examples. Individuals feel nurtured when you trust them to do their job well and focus on what they get right, not what they get wrong.

Decisive

Your ability to make decisions will improve with practice. In some situations you may be indecisive because you don't have enough information to hand and require more. In general, though, you have to be prepared not only to make a decision but also to take responsibility for it. If you choose to be in charge, the buck stops with you.

Organised

You have to be super-organised to be in charge. Don't attempt to leave things to memory; it really does help to write things down. Not only does this stop you forgetting it also allows you to prioritise tasks in order of importance.

Self-esteem

There is no doubt that getting a promotion is a boost to self-esteem. However, it should never be seen as a prop to base your self-esteem on. Good leaders – or potential leaders – can be attracted to things like financial security, respect, kudos and a sense of achievement, but the one quality they all possess is an underlying self-confidence that doesn't depend on any of these things. You have to work on developing this for yourself, and not rely on a job title to do it for you. I have recommended some good books on this subject in the Further Reading at the back of this book.

▪ Becoming Self-employed

Self-employment is not the same as running your own business. A large percentage of self-employed individuals don't run businesses, but hire out their services and skills to companies on short to medium-term contracts. Using contract workers and self-employed staff suits many companies, as it can be cheaper and more efficient to bring in outside experts, it provides flexibility and staff can be recruited for specific projects only.

Before considering the pros and cons of becoming self-employed, give some thought to the type of work you do or want to do. For example, in TV and the media a large percentage of staff are self-employed and working on short-term contracts – even if you want a full-time permanent position in such a field it can be difficult to find one. However, it does mean that regular, short-term recruitment takes place. If it's not the norm in your chosen area it may be an ongoing struggle to secure regular employment. You can get an idea what the situation is like by contacting the sort of companies that you would potentially be working for, and asking how many staff are full-time employees and how many are temporary outside staff. Be specific though. There's no point finding out that a company has 20 per cent outside staff if it relates to contract cleaners and your particular area is computer programming.

The following exercise will help you to assess your suitability for self-employment.

EXERCISE

To assess your suitability for self-employment read the following list of things you may be required to do and put a tick next to what you would feel comfortable with and prepared to take on:

- Handling your own accounts and making all necessary deductions, i.e. National Insurance, tax ☐
- Promoting and marketing yourself ☐
- Not having paid holidays and sickness cover ☐
- Not having a regular weekly or monthly salary ☐
- Not having job security ☐
- Not being limited to a fixed salary ☐
- Having more choice about the hours you work ☐
- Doing a variety of work for a number of companies ☐
- Not being as affected by or involved in office politics ☐
- Always being in the market for new opportunities ☐
- Able to use a wider variety of skills ☐

As you can see from the above list, when it comes to the pros and cons of self-employment versus employment, it's all a matter of perception. What one person would see as an advantage is a disadvantage to another. The deciding factor when assessing your suitability for self-employment is that you are aware of what is involved and that the pros outweigh the cons. Speaking as a self-employed person, I love not knowing what project I will be working on in six months' time or who I'll be coaching next. So much so that I never commit to a long-term project, because I love variety. But I have friends who tell me this would give them sleepless nights. They would hate not to be able to plan ahead or feel secure about their finances.

One of the great advantages of self-employment is that you can hugely increase your earning potential – after all, you don't have to wait around for annual salary reviews, you have far greater free-dom to negotiate your own rates of pay and you aren't tied to a grading or salary structure. But finances can also be one of the great disadvantages because payment is often irregular, companies can keep you waiting for months before settling an invoice, and unless you are constantly proactive about finding new work, your earnings will be very erratic.

Being self-employed can give you a lot of freedom about the work you choose to take on, how you prioritise your working day, and being able to negotiate your value and handle your own accounts. But many people prefer the discipline of working to set hours. Asking for a salary review and increase can be all too painful even once a year, never mind negotiating your value on a regular basis. And having a variable income and the responsibility of keeping accounts could cause huge headaches. It's all a matter of perception based on the sort of person you are. It can also be a matter of timing. I've met lots of people who have happily shifted between employment and self-employment, finding different things suit them at different times.

▪ Is the Risk Worth the Reward?

When it comes to running your own business, all successful people have this in common: not only are they prepared to take risks, they are also willing to take responsibility. Taking responsibility for success is easy, but few people want to risk being responsible for a failure.

It's hardly surprising when you think about the culture of shame that surrounds business failures in most European countries. In cultures of shame there is no recognition or respect for the courage, energy and imagination it takes simply to have a go. Effort and ideas alone are not rewarded – no matter how great. You are measured only on the end result, and you are either a winner or a loser. It's a harsh, black and white judgement system that doesn't encourage or reward innovation. By contrast, in America the only shame is never trying. Even if you fail you are still encouraged to have another go.

The most successful entrepreneurs like Richard Branson or Donald Trump, have had their share of business failures, but they refuse to be shamed out of trying again, and that's how they get to be successful. Not that this is easy. In the UK, many people are cynical and quick to pour cold water over new business ideas. Why do you think 57 per cent of Americans according to the GEM

(Global Entrepreneurship Monitor) say that they see a good opportunity to start a business in the next six months, compared to only 16 per cent in the UK? Yet the failure rate of start-ups is consistent – about 45 per cent across both countries. This suggests that people are more put off by cultural stigma than the statistical risk of business failure. It is true that 45 per cent is a high number, but 55 per cent is still higher!

If you do decide to go it alone, be prepared for the fact that everyone has an opinion on the subject. When I started my own business, I was met with a tide of negativism. Then, when my business made money and I won a few business awards people were quick to tell me that I was the sort of person who couldn't fail. Nonsense! It was just that their perceptions changed when I became associated with success.

The one thing that overwhelmingly influenced me to start my business was the feeling that I'd never know if I could make a go of something. Dealing with failure wasn't as scary as that. I think this is one of the best questions you can ask yourself if you are thinking of starting your own business. Would you rather deal with the consequences of never knowing if you could succeed in your own business or the consequences of a failed venture?

It isn't an easy question to answer. No one can guarantee you success in business, but equally they can't guarantee you failure. It's up to you to determine the difference between success and failure in business. You may receive your biggest rewards when other people think you are experiencing your biggest setback.

Knowing what rewards are the most important to you will help you decide if it's worth taking the risk. Study the list below of some commonly expressed rewards for starting your own business and compile your own list in order of importance.

► Making a lot of money

► Making more money than I make now

► Doing things my way

► Making a name for myself

► Proving I've got what it takes

► Learning and growing

- Overcoming challenges
- Pushing myself beyond my normal limitations
- Making a difference
- Expressing my creativity
- Incorporating my values into my working life
- Having more freedom of choice
- Gaining the respect of other people
- Creating new opportunities for other people
- Doing something I love
- Fulfilling my vocation
- Knowing I have the courage to take the risk.

▪ Being in Charge

Now we'll work through the Formula to see if you've got what it takes to be in charge, how you can increase your skills and if it's what you really want.

Focus

Focus on what the problem is and write it down in your journal. Be careful how you word your problem, as you don't want to block yourself from finding a solution. If you are being overlooked for promotion, don't list this as the problem because it's a symptom. Look beyond the symptom. Ask yourself: Have you established the criteria and objectives that have to be met, do you have the relevant experience, are you demonstrating the ability to deal with the responsibility? When it comes to being self-employed or running your own business it won't help to list problems like 'I don't know if I will get enough work or if my business will be successful.' You have to accept that there are no guarantees. The real problem could be fear of failure or taking a risk. You need to identify this in order to find a solution.

Organise

With every problem you list, organise your thoughts and feelings. So if it's promotion you want, be honest about why you want it and if you warrant it. Remind yourself what your qualifications, skills and experience are. What makes you the best person for the job? You may be prepared to do whatever it takes to increase your income, but if you work in a very people-oriented organisation your employer may feel that your motives are not in line with company culture. Equally, in a highly competitive organisation where results are predominantly measured on profit your people skills could be less valued. It's worth considering if you are best suited to promotion in your existing workplace or if your values and skills are better served elsewhere.

If you want to be self-employed or run your own business, again be clear about why. Try writing down a list to express your feelings. Begin each sentence with 'I feel. . .'. Your list could say: 'I feel comfortable with the thought of being self-employed, I feel motivated by the thought of running my own business, I feel optimistic at the thought of taking a risk.' These are all positive feelings and thoughts. You may also be coming up with negative ones. If so, ask yourself if this is what you really want. Is the timing right? Pursuing something you don't want won't make you happy and negative responses can be an indication of how you really feel.

Make a list of solutions to your problem. Seeing them in black and white makes it easier to determine if they are workable.

Review

What were your previous experiences like? Has getting a promotion been an ongoing challenge or have you progressed at a pace you have been happy with? Has anything happened suddenly to spur you on to getting a promotion – do you feel people the same age as you are progressing faster? Are there any familiar patterns that keep repeating? Why does self-employment or running your own business appeal? Were you unhappy working as an employee? Has it been a case of timing and gaining the right experience? By reviewing previous work experiences you will get an idea of how you have got to where you are now. From here you can review your current situation and decide what you want to do next.

Motivate

If you are doing what feels right for you, then you should feel motivated. It's OK to feel fear and apprehension, which are perfectly normal reactions to doing something different and moving outside your comfort zone. In order to stay motivated and not let fear take over, remind yourself daily what your goals are (see Chapter 2) and why you want to achieve them. You may also need to motivate other people. Perhaps your boss isn't prioritising your promotion. If so, don't go in complaining and trying to present your case. Your needs won't motivate other people, so focus on their needs. For example, a promotion may allow you to share some of the responsibility your boss has, take over a demanding project or deal with staff related issues. Think about what's relevant to them.

Being self-employed means motivating companies to hire you by showing them the advantages *to them* of using you. In business you have to motivate staff, customers, bank managers. The same rule applies – accommodate their needs if you want to motivate them.

Utilise

This is where you focus on your strengths and also work to convert any weaknesses into strengths. Remember, not admitting to a weakness is a bigger problem than the weakness itself. Utilise your contacts to network, get information and effect introductions. Create opportunities to demonstrate what you are good at.

Liberate

This is a really challenging one because there are so many limiting and false beliefs that hold people back from reaching their potential. See if any of the following statements sound familiar:

- 'I'm probably too nice a person to make a lot of money.'

- 'I could succeed if only people would give me a chance.'

- 'No one is willing to listen to my ideas.'

- 'I can't delegate work because the staff are incompetent.'

- 'My boss has got it in for me.'

- 'You can't succeed in business with the present economic climate/government.'

- 'It's harder for me because I'm a woman/ I'm the wrong social class/ I didn't go to the right school.'

- 'I've never had enough support or encouragement.'

Not only does this list contain limiting beliefs, it also contains excuses. If you are the right person to succeed then you won't make excuses. Holding negative beliefs can simply be a bad habit and, like any habit, it can be broken. The first step is to admit to the habit – then you can do something about it. Here are some coaching techniques you can use to liberate yourself.

▶ Be selective about the company you keep and the advice you take. Don't surround yourself with people who support your negativity. Look for people who will challenge your beliefs and push you outside your comfort zone. So, for example, if you said to a friend 'No one ever listens to my ideas' and their response was 'I know what you mean, I have the same problem', they are supporting your negative belief. Whereas, if they said 'That's not my experience' or 'Have you tried putting your ideas across in a different way?' they are challenging your belief and encouraging you to think again.

▶ Don't rely entirely on instinct or your initial reaction. Fear can cause you take the easy option – you think you are too nice a person to make a lot of money. This belief lets you off the hook – you don't even have to try! Every time an existing belief stops you making progress, look for evidence to disprove it. With this example, look for a role model, someone successful who you admire and believe is a nice person – it could be a colleague, family member or a celebrity.

Act

Enough of theory, it's time to take action. By now you should be clear about what you want and, by working through the various exercises in this chapter, have a plan of action. So, if you identified that you need feedback from a boss or guidelines on how your performance is measured, write a date in your diary when you're going to ask for it and make sure you follow through.

You may need information about registering yourself as self-employed, or need legal advice on starting a business. Find out where you can get this information from, and set yourself a deadline for getting it.

▪ Facing the Challenge

Finally, you have to 'face' the challenge. You should have worked through the Formula and taken action. Next comes the application, which will move you forward. These are things like meeting objectives, developing additional skills, making the move to self-employment, forming a company. Things will always change when you apply a new method, so if you're working through the Formula properly you should be having a new experience in your working life. When the same old experiences keep repeating you can guarantee that you are doing the same old things. Be vigilant and, if necessary, retrace your steps to make sure you have made changes. Now you can record your results.

▪ Coaching Review

► To be in charge you have to be prepared to work at it and fully understand what it takes.

► Regardless of how many skills you have, you can guarantee being in charge requires you to learn more.

► The sort of company you work for will influence the type of leader you become.

► You need to know why you want a promotion, self-employment or to run your own business.

► If you are being overlooked for promotion clarify what your objectives are, how your performance is measured, ask for feedback and find ways to turn a weakness into a strength.

► Make sure you have the skills required and are prepared to improve on them and gain more.

► The pros and cons of being self-employed versus employed is a matter of perception based on the sort of person you are.

► Would you rather deal with the consequences of never knowing if you could succeed in your own business or the consequences of a failed business venture?

► You have to decide if the risk of starting your own business is worth the rewards you seek.

CHAPTER SIX

How to Communicate and Negotiate Effectively

I N MANY WAYS, THIS chapter is the equivalent of a booster shot for every other chapter in this book. Because no matter what skills or techniques you master, they will all be enhanced by your ability to communicate well. I can't stress enough how important this is. Good communication skills can not only help you find, get and succeed at the job of your dreams, but can make the difference in almost any area of work – or life – you care to name.

Being able to communicate and negotiate effectively is crucial to forming successful relationships, not just at work but in every area of life. We live increasingly in a knowledge economy where ideas, knowledge and service – and the ability to communicate all three – are what we are all selling, no matter what business we're in. In the current world of work, good communicators will always come first, and presentation skills are at a premium.

This may sound like a daunting prospect to you, but it needn't be. As children we are all natural and spontaneous communicators. Unfortunately, that spontaneity often ends up being suppressed by our parents, by critical teachers and by bullying bosses. Becoming a good communicator very often means just relearning skills you already have. This chapter will show you how to communicate and negotiate effectively, as well as how to improve your presentation skills and stay calm and in control during high-stress moments like job interviews.

If the thought of presentations or public speaking fills you with terror, don't be too hard on yourself. Most of us have at least some degree of discomfort in that situation. The secret of success is actually quite simple: master some essential tricks and techniques, and then put in plenty of practice. A leading presentation coach provides the presentation techniques I will be discussing in this chapter, and I often refer my own clients to presentation experts when they suddenly find they are required to give a professional presentation without proper training. If this is a problem you face, be reassured that you can significantly polish up on your performance and learn skills that will greatly increase your levels of confidence.

▪ Communication Tips

Begin by thinking about what makes a good communicator. Perhaps you know someone that springs to mind? It could be a friend, a television presenter or a school teacher. There's not one thing that makes them good, but a number of factors, and by breaking them down you will be able to see exactly what they are and if there are any areas you need to brush up on to improve your own skills.

Here are some key factors.

Listening

Listening is top of the list. Usually we are so preoccupied by what we are going to say that we fail to give equal attention to what others say. Listening requires you to not only remain silent but also to absorb the information you are receiving and respond to it.

Misunderstandings arise when people talk at each other rather than to each other. When you listen to two people having a disagreement, one of the most notable things is how often they fail to give relevant feedback. It's like they are having separate conversations and are only tuned into their own, so they miss any common ground or points of agreement. To be a good listener you have to calm your own thoughts, stop thinking about what you want to say and concentrate on what the other person is saying. This can take practice, so even if you believe you have digested what is being said, double check by using questions to clarify it. Useful questions are, 'Would I be right in thinking. . .?' or 'Does that mean you think. . .?'.

Clarity

Mental and written preparation will boost your ability to deliver clear information. Try these techniques.

► Think about what you want to say: if it's an important conversation, make a few notes in advance.

► What is the purpose of your conversation?

► What is your desired outcome?

► Does the situation call for a formal or informal approach? Is it acceptable to chat away in a friendly manner? Or is a certain protocol required?

► Have a mental rehearsal in advance. Be sure to highlight the points you want to emphasise and not get caught up in a lengthy dialogue that requires the listener to decipher the relevant points.

► Use positive emotions like enthusiasm to reinforce a message, not negative ones like anger, which can lead to confrontation.

► Concentrate on getting your message across rather than trying to sound clever. Some situations will obviously require you to demonstrate your knowledge, but you can still maintain clarity without resorting to convoluted jargon or waffling. Be specific.

Eye Contact

Maintaining good eye contact confirms your interest, sincerity and confidence. Avoid staring; this is unnerving and can send out the wrong signals. Remember to blink, lower your eyes briefly to relax them, then bring them back to the person you are talking to. Failing to make eye contact can send out signals that you are either nervous, have something to hide, or that you are insincere and not confident about the information you are relaying.

Body Language

Research claims that we give out more than 50 per cent of our message through our body language. When you are feeling relaxed, your body adopts a natural stance. When you're nervous, you will physically tense up and become prone to fidgeting, crossing your arms, biting your nails or bottom lip, and shifting your weight from one foot to the other.

Practise in front of a mirror so that you become used to using body language that looks relaxed even when you don't feel it. Before you start, breathe in through your nose and out through your mouth a few times. Give your arms and legs a shake, so they don't look rigid. Place your feet slightly apart and balance your weight equally on both feet. Imagine you have to complain about something, then make your complaint out loud into the mirror.

Make a note of your reactions during difficult conversations or situations, then make a conscious effort to correct any inappropriate movements.

Smiling

Responding with a smile shows you are receptive to information, and makes you look interested and friendly. A smile must be genuine, otherwise it can look like a sneer or as if you're being smug. In formal conversations people often want to be taken seriously, but a serious expression can look overly stern. If smiling isn't appropriate you can still maintain an open and relaxed-looking face. All it needs is a bit of practice and your ally, the mirror. Study your face. If you have two vertical lines between your eyebrows then clearly you are prone to frowning. Facial expressions are habitual and like any habit they can be broken. The next time you are required to concentrate, whether you're watching TV, working at a computer or reading, place your index finger and second finger between your eyebrows. If you find the eyebrows knitted together then gently ease them apart. In the process you will find that your forehead muscles have to relax, along with your eyes, cheeks and mouth muscles. Do this regularly and your face will begin to get used to the feeling, so when your face tenses you'll automatically sense it.

Content

Effective communicators always fill their conversation with more positive content than negative. Even when they have to communicate something inherently negative they avoid blame, criticism, gossip and personal remarks. The next time you are having a conversation listen very carefully to how much of your content is positive. Look out for comments like, 'I don't like . . .', 'The problem with . . .', 'What annoys me is . . .', 'I'm fed up with . . .', which are negative. Convert these statements into positive phrases by changing them to 'I would prefer. . .', 'The problem could be solved by. . .', 'What would please me is. . .', I don't want to repeat this situation and the way forward would be to. . .'.

When clients come to see me, for the most part they describe themselves as positive thinkers and communicators, but this isn't always the case. Some of them have unconsciously developed a bad habit of thinking and communicating negatively. A useful tip to see if you have room for improvement is to take note of how many friends you have who always moan when you talk to them and how many whingeing work colleagues make a beeline for you. As a rule negative communicators are less drawn to positive ones because they don't get the feedback they are after. They don't want a positive spin on things – they actually want your agreement that things are as bad as they say. Don't get pulled into their negativity. Deflect them with questions like, 'What would be the best possible outcome for you?' or 'How can you make things work for you?'.

Tone of Voice

Content matters, but *how* you say something is just as important as *what* you say – 37 per cent of your message comes just from your tone of voice, according to research. We have all listened to someone relaying an argument or disagreement and wondered what all the fuss is about. Equally, when someone is telling us about a partner complimenting them or a boss offering praise we can struggle to hear how the content of the words results in such pleasure. The whole point is that unless you actually hear it you don't appreciate the powerful nuances of conversation. A simple 'Well done', delivered in a warm and sincere voice, is more powerful than stronger words of praise that sound sarcastic or insincere.

Our individual antennae are usually very receptive to incoming messages. You may be quick to hear a sarcastic, indifferent, bored and irritated tone, yet less aware when you deliver one. A sign that all is not well in your own communication is constant confrontation, feeling misunderstood and being unable to form close relationships at work or in your social life. Never assume other people 'should know' what you mean – as a rule they don't.

People interpret what you say by your tone of voice. A useful exercise is to tape your voice and listen to the recording. Significantly, the common response to hearing ourselves on tape is, 'I can't believe that's what I sound like.' And, of course, that's exactly how you sound. So make sure your tone is reflective of how you actually feel and want to come across.

▪ The Effective Negotiator

The list above covers the basic skills of good communication. There is also one advanced skill – that of the effective negotiator. This demonstrates well-developed interpersonal skills and goes a long way to paving positive relationships at work. To develop this skill successfully you have to want to go the extra mile, because it really challenges your levels of tolerance, understanding, forgiveness and acceptance of others. It requires you to be non-judgemental and create the space for compromise. What makes this a particularly difficult challenge is that you can often feel like the only person creating this space.

When my clients take responsibility for improving their communication skills and their awareness of good communication increases they also develop a heightened awareness of bad communication. Now, this can be very frustrating. As my client Joan put it 'Every day when I walk into the office and listen to other people it's like, spot the obvious mistake. How can people be so unaware and indifferent to how they come across?'. But being unaware does not always equate to indifference. I have mediated disputes within companies and my experience is that both parties believe they are right. Yes, I do encounter the odd vindictive individual, but it is the exception. Generally both parties are so locked into their own side of the story that they just don't hear anyone else.

What never works in this situation is to make the other person wrong. Yet that's what most people do, with comments like 'You never listen', 'The problem with you is . . .', 'Why do you always have to be so. . .'. We are all guilty of reacting in this way. Emotions run high during disputes, and attack is often used as a defensive action. My role as a mediator is an easy one, because as an outside observer I don't have the emotional involvement and this lets me see both sides clearly. Your role as a negotiator to your own situation means that you are also affected by your emotions and have to find a way to distance yourself from them to find a solution. You can use the Formula to do this next time you need to be a negotiator to your own situation.

EXERCISE

This exercise will show you how to be your own negotiator.

Focus

Keep your focus on what your objectives are and what you want to achieve. Be sure to say what these are, because there is no room for progress when two parties are working towards completely different objectives. State your case without making the other party wrong. Avoid any comments that sound like attack or criticism because they will bring out negative emotions, which can result in a slanging match and prevent you from behaving in an objective manner. Work situations call for a professional approach and while you may feel passionate about things you have to be careful this emotion does not bring about an irrational argument. Try to stick to objective facts.

Organise

You have to come up with a solution that will work for both parties. Ask yourself, how can I achieve what I want without overriding the feelings of others? If you are really struggling to come up with a solution, try this technique. You'll need the assistance of a trusted friend or partner here. Relay to them your situation in as much detail as possible. Then try some role reversal. Get them to relay the problem back to you as if they are the person experiencing it. Now try and offer them some solutions. You will be surprised how effective this technique can be, as it often allows you to step outside your problem and, by losing the emotional attachment, see a solution that was not previously obvious.

Review

Have you considered all options? Don't forget it takes two to have a dispute. In some situations the best option can be walking away. It depends on what's at stake, and how it affects you. Has this ever happened to you in the past? If so, what did you learn from that experience? How can you do things differently this time? Can you avoid this in the future?

Motivate

Make a list of the points both parties agree on and emphasise them. You may be motivated to negotiate a mutual solution, but you may also have to motivate the other party by demonstrating the common ground. Constantly emphasising the differences won't motivate anyone. Get the other party to expand on their ideas by showing interest and asking questions. Perhaps they haven't thought things through clearly and an open discussion may make them aware of this. Do not let the focus be on attack, defence and making the other person wrong.

Utilise

Your strength is that you want to move forward so avoid questions that keep you blocked, such as 'Why are they treating me this way?'. Better questions include 'How can I make this work for me?', 'What concessions can I make without compromising my values?', 'How can I demonstrate my commitment to finding a mutual solution?'.

Liberate

It may seem liberating to be proved right, but it takes great personal courage to admit you are wrong. Always question the beliefs that contributed to the opinions you have formed, and ask whether or not they are limiting or misplaced beliefs. Put yourself in the other person's place and think about the sort of beliefs they may hold. You may not agree with them, but understanding their conviction encourages respect.

Act

A negotiator's actions must be constructive, not destructive. The temptation is to strengthen your position by weakening the other party's position. But this isn't negotiation; it's a power struggle. I often hear a person described as a 'tough negotiator', which is a bit of a contradiction in terms. It suggests a rigid, fixed approach, with little room for compromise. Think carefully about taking any action that involves pulling rank or showing disregard for another person's opinion.

A dispute arose at a restaurant because the head chef wanted to promote buffet lunches, which he believed most customers preferred. The restaurant manager wanted to promote the higher priced fixed lunches, as they were more profitable. The dispute went on for weeks, until finally the manager pulled rank and removed the buffet lunch from the menu.

The manager contacted me the following week, because the dispute was now worse than ever. He was having a major problem with customers complaining about the length of time they had to wait for food. The standard of food was excellent, but customers had limited time for lunch. The head chef was adamant that he was going as fast as he could and blamed the delay on the low staff cover at lunchtime.

I sat them both down and asked the manager why he was so keen on the fixed lunches, because it was important to establish the reason for his objectives. He said they were more profitable. I then asked him what profit targets he needed to reach. He gave me the figure and explained that they had been below target and the restaurant owner was considering staff cutbacks to compensate. The head chef had no idea of this; his objectives were to give customers what they wanted by catering for the fast turnaround at lunchtime.

I didn't have to say much more as both parties suddenly had a new perspective on the situation. The conversation that followed between them went well. The head chef had made some good observations, which the manager now noted. Time was important to the customers but the chef could now see profit had to be considered. Between them they found a workable solution, and the buffet menu was reintroduced with the inclusion of either a half or full bottle of wine.

Within a few weeks two-thirds of the customers were having the buffet lunch, with the remaining customers opting for the fixed menu lunches. There were no lengthy delays in service and restaurant profits were up. And there was a bonus. The manager told me that the atmosphere between the staff had greatly improved and he was receiving lots of good suggestions for improving service and profit.

The key to this case study is to understand the role of the negotiator. They don't have to determine who is right or wrong. Maybe the manager didn't demonstrate good managerial skills by pulling rank; maybe the head chef was digging his heels in and deliberately creating a delay. The bottom line is that they both had pretty plausible reasons for behaving the way they did and they both had equal support from their respective staff. The secret lies in giving both parties a way forward, which is not achieved by making someone wrong. Trying to create a winner and loser will only keep the dispute going or result in a new one occurring. The main negotiation points to keep in mind are as follows.

► Effective negotiation means finding a mutually acceptable way forward for both parties.

► Don't attempt to make the other person wrong.

► The other party is likely to feel as strongly as you do.

► You want to have your opinions respected, so be sure that you are respecting other people's.

► This is not a point-scoring exercise. A sign that you are not in negotiation mode is when you start to accumulate evidence and support that you are in the right.

► You have to show that you are flexible and prepared to make compromises, otherwise why should the other party?

▪ Communicating Well in an Interview

Even the most confident people can find an interview daunting. By preparing in advance you can look and sound confident even if you don't feel it. Nerves are actually useful when used properly. They can energise your performance and keep you on your toes. Problems arise when they take over and prevent you performing to the best of your ability. Interviews are a very unnatural format, making most people feel scrutinised and on trial. Good preparation minimises these more negative aspects and greatly increases both your confidence and performance. Here is a preparation checklist to help you.

Preparation Checklist

▶ Along with knowing the time and date of an interview, it's important to check the location, especially if you are not familiar with it. When travel is involved, check out alternative modes of transport. If your first choice is to travel by train, make sure you know alternative bus routes in case of any delay. If you are driving by car allow plenty of time, check out alternative routes in case of hold-ups and find out if there is parking or whether to leave your car.

▶ Gather as much information as possible about the company and job, for example, job description, how long the company has been in business, annual reports, reputation, products and services. Your local library or the Internet offer useful sources of information. Ideally the interview should be a time for you and a prospective employer to get to know each other better. Don't waste your or an employer's time having an interview for a job and company you know little about. Make a list of the questions you need answers to and get as many answers as possible in advance.

▶ Prepare in advance everything you have to bring with you on the day such as CVs and references.

▶ One of the most common questions in an interview is, 'Tell me about yourself.' Rehearse your answer prior to the interview.

Remember the interviewer is specifically interested in why you would be right for the job, so answers must be relevant and show you in a favourable light. Make a list of all your strong points, skills and experience, and keep reading it aloud a few days before the interview. Don't just quote a list of achievements, relate them to your personal skills, so, if you were promoted to customer service manager in your previous job, emphasise your skills of helping others and problem solving.

► Dress appropriately for the interview. This is not the time to try out a new outfit, as you may not feel comfortable in it. Nerves can bring on excessive perspiration, which can be minimised by wearing fabrics like cotton next to the skin. White shirts don't show perspiration!

► Arrive early so you have time to visit the bathroom and check your appearance. Notify the receptionist of your arrival, purpose of visit and who you are there to see.

► Watch your body language. Keep good eye contact, don't fidget, fold your arms or slouch in your chair.

► Listen to each question carefully. Don't waffle or go off on a tangent. Having said that, simple yes and no answers will not demonstrate your ability as a good communicator.

► The interviewers can see your qualifications on your CV. In an interview situation they are assessing other skills. Therefore, you have to relate this to what the job requires and take it as the opportunity to demonstrate them. So make sure it shows if you are good at thinking on your feet, friendly, enthusiastic, keen to take on a challenge, flexible, creative, articulate, able to generate ideas . . .

► Don't get caught off guard by an informal interview. Some companies deliberately conduct informal interviews because the candidate is likely to reveal more. That's OK if what you reveal demonstrates a professional attitude.

► Prioritise the order of questions you ask. Always ask about the company first in terms of their goals, objectives and any challenges they face. Then ask about how your performance will be measured and objectives that are specific to your job. Leave questions like terms and conditions until last. Even in very competitive workplaces no interviewer wants to see that your top priority is what's in it for you.

Interviews won't always be for a job with a different company. Promotion may involve you having an internal interview, in which case you should be just as well prepared. There is little room for complacency and you may well be constantly assessed on your ability to communicate and present.

▪ Presentation Skills

Even with the current emphasis on presentation skills, there are still many companies and occasions where staff are thrown in at the deep end with no training or guidance. No matter how good you are at your job, or how knowledgeable and competent in your subject, it's worth noting that presentation requires specialised skills, so don't be hard on yourself if you find this a challenge.

Presentation coach Ian Oliver recommends the following five top tips for public speaking.

1. **Preparation** Always prepare your talk in advance and write it down. Begin by making bullet points of what you want to say, then expand on this. Stories, anecdotes and analogies are easier to remember, and a great way to get a message across. They also help you to personalise your talk and relate to your audience.

2. **Rehearsal** Have several rehearsals and a full dress rehearsal (wearing what you are planning to wear at the talk). Use a full-length mirror to check your appearance and body language. Time your speech.

3. **Connecting** Your audience has to hear you, believe you and understand you.

   ► *Hear you:* this means projecting your voice or using a microphone and having clarity of voice.

   ► *Believe you:* your speech/presentation should be genuine and authentic. Use your voice to deliver the message, so if you find something exciting – sound excited, if you are delivering praise or a heartfelt message, allow some emotion into your voice.

▶ *Understand you:* a simple, well-delivered message is much more powerful than convoluted waffle. You want your audience to retain information, so start by telling them what you are going to tell them, then tell it to them, and lastly sum up by telling them what you have told them.

4. **Content** The content of your talk must be appropriate to the occasion. If you want to add humour, an amusing story or anecdote is easier to deliver than a joke or one-liner. It takes timing and practice to tell a joke well, so this is not the time to try out your latest gag.

5. **Nerves** Even the professionals get nervous. Accept this as a natural part of the process. A burst of nervous energy can be channelled into a great performance.

Dealing with Nerves

Because nerves can get out of control, Ian Oliver uses a variety of methods to counteract symptoms like a rapid heartbeat, excessive sweating, shaking, dry mouth and throat, and the much-dreaded stomach upset.

First, list the symptoms that you tend to experience. We all react differently when nervous and everyone's body responds differently to methods of counteracting nerves. You may need to try a few techniques to achieve the best balance for you.

- Avoid stimulating drinks that contain caffeine, along with spicy or high-fibre foods on the day of your presentation, and the day before.

- Eat little and often to combat stomach upsets and digestive problems.

- If you are prone to shaking, hold something like your notes, which you can alternate between hands, or make use of visual aids, to allow you to move about during your presentation.

- In most work situations alcohol is an absolute no no. Have a glass of water on hand to combat a dry mouth and throat.

It may help to unload your nerves just prior to a presentation. To do this you can telephone a friend or talk to a close work colleague – you will need to prepare them in advance so they know what to do. Tell your friend or colleague exactly how you are feeling. Getting things off your chest can be a great relief and it's OK to admit you are feeling terrified, worried you will dry up, make a fool of yourself or forget what you have to say. Once you have done this your friend or colleague can run through with you a checklist that you have supplied them with in advance. The checklist should cover all the things you have done in preparation, such as your talk, notes and bullet points in case you forget or lose your train of thought, visual aids (if you are using them), handouts if required, and so on. Both nerves and fear can be irrational, and saying them aloud diffuses much of the emotional steam behind them. Complete it with a rational reminder of how much preparation you have actually done. That way you can begin your talk with rational thoughts at the forefront of your mind.

▪ Communication Challenge

To conclude this chapter I would like you to set yourself a communication challenge. Select something that you would normally avoid or certainly find difficult. This could involve you volunteering to give a presentation, asking your boss for feedback, a pay rise, resolving a dispute or having a conversation with a colleague that involves you doing most of the listening. It's important to tackle a difficult area so that you can overcome any weaknesses as well as build on any strengths. The following technique will provide you with a solid structure to work through this process.

EXERCISE

1. Begin by setting yourself a goal, either from the selection given above or think of something different.

2. Make a list of all the things that have caused a problem/
   block in the past. Perhaps you don't have good
   presentation skills, or you're afraid of receiving negative
   feedback or being criticised. Next to each problem you
   have listed write down the benefits of achieving your goal,
   under the following headings:

GOAL	PROBLEM/ BLOCK	BENEFIT OF ACHIEVING MY GOAL
Give a presentation	I don't have good presentation skills	Improve my confidence Improve my career prospects
Ask my boss for feedback	Afraid of criticism	Demonstrate to my boss my enthusiasm to improve my performance I will know my strengths and any weaknesses to improve on
Resolve a dispute	I lose my temper easily	I will stop repeating the same mistakes and move forward

3. Each problem/block you have identified will highlight your
   weak area of communication and show you what action to
   take. So you may need to read some good books on
   presentation or take a training course. If you are afraid or
   upset by criticism, accept this as a perfectly normal
   reaction – none of us likes it. However, you can still be a
   good communicator by making a commitment not to react
   defensively and aggressively. Listen to what is being said
   and, if necessary, ask for some time to think through what
   has been said. This is your cooling off period; your first
   reaction and emotion can come from fear – fear of not
   being liked – not being good enough. Let these negative
   emotions defuse and then consider if what has been said is
   valid. Ask yourself how you can improve. How can you use

the remarks in a constructive way? A useful tip to remember is that when you fear receiving feedback to the point that you never ask for it, you are your own worst critic because you doubt your own performance. By hearing it from someone else you are not confirming your fears but rather moving forward from denial. You need to acknowledge and address a weakness to turn it into a strength.

4. Don't react on negative emotions. Apply the rule of 'monopoly', which is saying to yourself I don't have a monopoly on feeling upset, angry, frustrated, afraid – in fact any negative emotion you care to mention. Everyone feels negative emotions, but what makes the difference is not acting on them because negative actions produce negative results. How you communicate is the biggest yardstick other people have to gauge the sort of person you are. Few people are either insightful enough or have the training to see beyond negative communication coming from hurt, pain and confusion. It's worth remembering this because all the things you dislike seeing in other people can become manifested in your own communication and behaviour when you react on negative emotions. A good communicator moves themselves and others forward by keeping their reactions and communication positive. Good questions and statements include:

- ► What would you like me to do?

- ► I'm sorry you feel this way. What would make you feel better about the situation?

- ► May I make a suggestion?

- ► What do you think/feel?

- ► I'm open to any suggestions/ideas you have

- ► Thank you for listening/talking to me

- ► I appreciate your feedback/comments.

▪ Facing the Challenge

Finally, you need to 'face' the challenge and record the results in your journal. Work through the Formula, then the application, which is the doing part of the process. In this case it may involve trying new methods of communication, offering solutions not problems and keeping conversations positive. Application will always promote change and as this occurs you can record the results.

▪ Coaching Review

► Effective communication and negotiation is crucial to forming successful relationships.

► You have the potential to be a great communicator. All it takes is practice and familiarising yourself with skills you were born with.

► Break down all the contributing factors – like listening, body language, tone of voice, eye control – that make a good communicator so you can see what areas you need to brush up on.

► To be a successful negotiator you have to go the extra mile because it requires well-developed interpersonal skills and tests your levels of tolerance, understanding, forgiveness, acceptance and compassion.

► When negotiating you have to find a mutually acceptable solution for all parties, which isn't achieved by making the other party wrong and yourself right.

► When it comes to public speaking, even the professionals get nervous. You can channel nerves into a high energy performance.

► Always remember how you feel when you are on the receiving end of negative communication and make a commitment not to repeat it.

CHAPTER SEVEN

How to Double Your Income

I F YOU'VE MANAGED TO read the book so far without giving this chapter a sneak preview, well done! I know what a siren call the title is likely to be. Money is one of the most important and emotionally charged issues of our lives, and it doesn't necessarily make us greedy or materialistic. Money happens to be our major means of exchange, and it's what dictates much of our life and lifestyle. We don't have to love money for its own sake to appreciate its value, and none of us can deny its importance.

Of course, the prospect of doubling your income is very appealing and that's what this chapter is about. I want to show you what makes you valuable to an employer and how you can increase your value. In this context I'm talking about financial worth. What this chapter is not about is working harder, working longer hours or get-rich-quick schemes. And while most of us might like to earn more money, there are often other values that determine the choices we make at work, that also directly affect our income levels, so I'll be discussing these too. I will also be asking you to examine your relationship to money and how much control you have over it. My role is to give you the coaching techniques to help you do this, not to influence or judge your choice, but to enable you to highlight all your options so you can make a choice that's right for you.

I've had experiences with money from both sides of the fence. I watched my parents work their entire adult lives just to keep their heads above water. My father was a manual worker who eventually had to retire on a disability pension after years of intense physical labour. My mother was skilled but chose vocational jobs that never paid very much. Although I didn't set out with a primary goal of having a high income, I earned more in a few years than they did in their combined lifetimes. All I did was apply my skills in a different way. And that's what I want to show you how to do.

▪ Will More Money Make You Happy?

Let me start with one very important point. Like you I have values and what I do and how I do it matters to me, and I found a way of doing things on my own terms that made money. That's exactly what you have to do, because you won't be happy making money doing something that you don't like or that gives you a serious value conflict.

It's easy enough to think of possible business ventures if you try to, but that doesn't mean you should always pursue them. You may find quick ways of making money or opportunities with potentially high rewards, but they could involve working in a way that doesn't suit you, or they could be high risk or have no long-term prospects. Changing jobs can be financially advantageous, but again there can be factors like relocation, job security and finding the right organisation for you to take into account.

You already know how important motivation is from working through the Formula. But are you *sufficiently* motivated by money to focus your skills and career on maximising your income, probably at the expense of some other aspects of your work? I once employed a sales rep who spent more time with each client than any of her colleagues. Even after she'd completed a sale, she liked to talk to the client, check that they were happy and generally keep in touch. She didn't get any extra payment for this, and if she'd spent the extra time chasing new clients she could potentially have earned more commission. But forming strong customer relationships and personal interaction motivated her even more than making another sale.

Making money isn't difficult, but it does depend on many conditions, some of which you may feel fine about, and some of which you may not. Money matters to all of us, but it's crucial to recognise that money may not be the thing that makes you feel most happy and successful. You may benefit more – and feel genuinely richer – from satisfying other values.

▪ Assessing Your Financial Needs

Before you start the process of doubling your income, you have to ask yourself what you are doubling it for. We all have very different ideas about how much money is enough. Your relationship to money and whether or not you are capable of controlling it lies deep within your values and beliefs.

Perhaps you desire money, but resent other people for having it. Maybe you view it as the thing that will set you free, but at the same time the thing that keeps you imprisoned, trapped by the need to keep earning more and more.

Lack of money causes anxiety, frustration, embarrassment, fear and stress. Most people have experienced financial worries at some time in their lives, and for many it's an ongoing concern. Others spend more than they earn and increasingly rely on credit cards, loans and overdrafts to support their lifestyle. That's not because they're all irresponsible and incapable of judicious financial planning. It's just that they adopt a head-in-the-sand approach. Pull their heads out of the sand and they know the theory of sensible money management – it's practising it that gives them problems.

If you double your income, but fail to control your finances you can guarantee that you'll double your outgoings, which basically brings you back to where you started. Yes, you may be able to buy a bigger house or take a better holiday, but you'll still experience the same financial worries. Whatever stage you are at, you need to assess your immediate situation to establish what your needs are. You can do this by working through the Formula and learning how to apply your financial know-how to your own situation.

▪ The Formula for Financial Success

Focus

Think about your existing financial position and make a list of any problems that exist like:

► being in debt

► unable to save

- spending beyond your means
- not being able to have the sort of lifestyle you desire
- not enough money to meet regular outgoings
- habit of 'binge-spending' – such as blowing a whole month's salary within the first few days of being paid
- compulsive saving and planning for the future, never enjoying money in the present
- ignoring or denying financial problems, such as debt.

Organise

Now is the time to organise your finances and begin the process of taking control. Start by listing all your monthly outgoings. I've done this back-to-basics exercise with numerous clients, and apart from the obvious expenses like mortgages or rent, utilities (gas, electricity, water and telephone) and travel expenses, I've found that few people have any idea what they are actually spending their money on each month until they sit down and itemise things. When you have completed this list you will have a much more realistic idea of how much disposable income you actually have.

So, if you're looking to double your income you should now be able to see the areas you need or want the money for. The idea is to get ahead and have more than you need to cover the basics. You should be aiming for sufficient earnings to enable you to save at least 10 per cent of your annual income.

Review

What have your finances been like to date? Has your standard of living improved? Have you increased your income only to have the same financial worries? Are there any patterns that keep repeating? You don't want to duplicate any previous mistakes so good review questions include:

- 'How will I do things differently this time?'
- 'What steps can I take to ensure that an increased income will give me what I want?'

- 'What am I prepared to do to earn more money?'

- 'How can I get the balance right between enjoying my income and saving?'

Motivate

Having financial goals is the best way to keep you motivated to improve your situation. Don't set a negative goal like 'Get out of debt', because you will stay focused on the problem. Think about the outcome you want:

► to increase your savings

► to generate more disposable income

► to have enough money to get married

► to have sufficient income to start a family.

► to save enough money for a great holiday

► to build up an 'emergency' fund

► to be able to buy/upgrade my home.

Remember you have to really want something in order to achieve it.

Utilise

Your strength could be that you are very good with money and don't spend beyond your means. So, if you increase your income you'll immediately see the benefit. However, if that's not the case you can turn a past weakness into a strength by admitting it and doing something about it such as paying all your bills by direct debit or standing order, or opening a savings account.

Liberate

The beliefs you hold could be preventing you from having the sort of income you really want. Be careful about harbouring deeply lodged feelings such as, 'I am just not the sort of person who will ever have money', 'Only ruthless people make money' or 'Making money makes you a less nice person.' It's also useful to question your attitude to people who have money. Be really honest with yourself. Do you resent them? Feel envious? Begrudge them what they have? These are all attitudes that will hold you back and can result in you sabotaging your own attempts to prosper.

Act

There are lots of actions you can take. You can draw up a monthly spending and saving plan, detailing where you have to spend and where you can save. It could be that you see an area that you can make a saving in and then want to invest some money, which is one way to increase your income. So you'll need to research possible investment opportunities. Or your action could be to get some information about the types of job and companies that pay well – like sales positions that offer high commission, or a job with a bonus linked to performance.

If you have real money worries you have to act to take the pressure off before moving forward. You can get some professional financial advice if things really seem to be out of control. Organisations like the Citizens' Advice Bureau, or most local government or council offices, provide a free service, as do many banks. It's often easier for an outsider to see some practical measures you can take to ease the stress. When financial pressure dictates every decision you make it's impossible to make the best ones. There has to be long-term financial planning in place so that you are not tempted only to pursue what looks like the most lucrative options. The workplace is full of grasshoppers jumping from one thing to the next in the hope of making big money. This is a reactive position and not one that allows you to think things through clearly. You may not need to leave your job or workplace at all. Before you make any decisions, you need to take a good look at your skills and how to make them work harder for you.

▪ Facing the Challenge

Now that you have used the formula it's time to face the challenge.

(Formula + Application + Change + Experience) = results

Just to remind you how this works, the application is the bit in the middle when you are doing something like organising your finances, talking to a financial adviser or your bank manager, cutting up your credit cards if that's the best way to stop you over-spending. Once you have progressed to the application your situation will change. Even if this area has been a disaster for you in the past you will still see positive changes such as not getting into any further debt, feeling more in control of the situation, having the benefit of good financial advice. And if necessary changing both your attitude and approach to handling your finances.

When it comes to experience this is ongoing. But remember you are looking for new and positive experiences and to break any negative patterns. Don't forget to record your results. Finances pose a tough challenge for lots of people and it's easy to feel both isolated and overwhelmed when you tackle this area. That's why it's so important to remind yourself of every improvement you make from feeling more confident, less stressed to clearing your debts and having a new saving plan.

▪ The Value of Having Skills

I often hear it said that if you increase your skills and do something that 'adds value' you'll be duly rewarded. But it's not quite that straightforward.

There are many highly skilled, vocational types of work that don't receive the financial rewards they deserve, just as there are hard, labour-intensive jobs that pay badly. Public sectors like the health service and education have fixed pay structures. You won't receive a bonus for making more patients better or increasing your levels of productivity. If teachers and college lecturers took their skills into the commercial market place they could double or even treble their income.

Again, this comes back to your values. If financial rewards are a major priority there are sectors of the workplace that could leave you feeling unacceptably undervalued because their remuneration packages are quite small. You need to take this into account when you are choosing a job or considering if the rewards are sufficient for you to remain in your current position.

The private sector, of course, is often more lucrative and provides more opportunity for financial gain. Private companies are usually funded by profit and if you can increase that profit you stand a good chance of being rewarded. But not all of these companies are bursting with opportunity and there are those that don't share their revenue with employees, regardless of the contribution they make.

So increasing your income is not always a simple matter of increasing your skills or working for a high profit-making company.

The answer lies with you, your attitudes and the way you apply your skills and experience.

Your Skills Audit

You can begin the process of using your skills differently with a skills audit. Make a list of each skill you have, then write as many examples as possible of how you have used these skills at work. Some examples might be:

SKILL	COMMERCIAL APPLICATION
Marketing	In my last job I identified a previously untapped market for sales. Over 6 months I developed this area and increased profits by 15 per cent
Accountancy	I saved my firm £20,000 a year by spotting that they were paying delivery charges on stationery orders under £100. Now orders are placed monthly and there is no delivery charge
Administration	Sales orders were being delayed by processing through head office. I moved the order line directly to the warehouse, which speeded up and increased sales, and gave staff at head office more time to process new accounts

If you haven't worked before or are returning to work after a lengthy gap you can still prepare a skills audit by listing qualifications you have and hobbies. Don't overlook the potential of turning a hobby into a full-time occupation. Here are some examples to get you started.

SKILL	APPLICATION
Gardening	I have extensive knowledge of plants and vegetables and have won several prizes for my allotment.
DIY	I have a flair for DIY and have successfully upholstered furniture, mastered complicated painting techniques.
Fund raising	As an active member of my community I have organised charity fun runs, sponsored walks and local fêtes.

Now ask yourself how you could use your skills. Could you present them better to get a promotion in your current position or to get a better new job? Could you use them to become self-employed? Maybe you could present your skills as a way to get a bonus-linked salary? Can you use your organisational skills in a work environment? Once you see clearly what you can do, you can start to plan ways to either improve and increase your skills or make them work harder for you.

▪ Brains Versus Brawn

We all have our talents but, plainly, certain things come more easily to some people than they do to others. Remember those classmates at school who seemed to have been granted with more than their fair share of natural ability? Many people see this as somehow unfair, and believe that they didn't start out on a level playing field. They were never encouraged as a child, they were pushed too hard and put under too much pressure, or they were never given a chance, or a parent, partner or a boss stopped them from achieving what they wanted . . .

It's quite easy to get locked into these beliefs and carry them with you throughout your life. But being plagued by self-doubt, blaming other people or believing that you are at a natural disadvantage will do nothing for you except hold you back. It's not the most talented individuals who succeed more often – it's the most determined. Haven't we all known highly intelligent individuals who have never achieved financial success?

To a large extent, success is not so much a matter of what you have, but of what you choose to do with it. Making money doesn't make you the best, the cleverest or the most astute. It simply shows that if that's what you decide you want then you have created the circumstances to get it. Regardless of what got you to this point in time you can still progress on a level playing field because there are no real limitations, only the ones you decide to put in place. You take what you have and find a way to maximise it.

For example, the UK Association of Graduate Recruiters' Graduate Salaries and Vacancies 1999 survey found that, in order of priority, the skills most in demand are: team working, interpersonal skills, motivation and enthusiasm, flexibility, customer orientation, business awareness, problem solving, planning and organisation, and numeracy. Don't you think it's interesting how much emphasis there is on what could be defined as life skills or experience, as opposed to academic skills? At graduate recruitment level academic aptitude is a basic requirement to getting your foot on the ladder. It doesn't set you apart from other recruits. What makes you more attractive to an employer is work-based experience.

Now as a graduate you could feel short-changed by this. Especially if you feel the goalposts had been moved after years of study. At the start of your degree there may have been no emphasis on work experience, so perhaps taking a year out or vocational work didn't look as useful as studying for higher marks. But you can't focus on the negative. If you want to get ahead you have to look at the here and now. Your goal might have been to get a degree and now you have to decide what to do with it. No one can take away your knowledge and your next move is to find a job that allows you to use it to your advantage. Do you want to use it to make money quickly? Are you prepared to start on a lower income and progress through a company pay structure or do you want to consider other options?

If you are not a graduate, you may have opted for the route of working your way up from the bottom by gaining experience. This has great value, but to progress further you may now need more academic skills. This can cause a block, especially if it's a long time since you went through the formal learning process or previously had a bad experience with education. There are those who learn much better on their feet, when the theory is very much tied up with the practical application. However, you may not be crediting yourself for the academic skills you have already acquired, and could make the mistake of thinking you are starting from scratch, when you're already well progressed. This is what happened to my client Kevin.

Kevin came to see me because he was so terrified of going on the managerial course he had been offered that he seriously considered declining the offer. Having worked his way up from unloading the vans for a stationery company to warehouse supervisor, Kevin was highly thought of by his firm. One of the company directors had taken him aside and said how the company would really benefit from someone like Kevin in management. The director gave him a prospectus for the managerial training course, with a personal recommendation to secure him a place.

Kevin showed me the prospectus and said, 'I'm really embarrassed, I haven't got a clue what half this stuff means.' I reassured him that neither did I – like many similar training brochures it was full of unnecessary jargon. I asked Kevin to tell me what his existing job entailed and we had a lot of fun converting his descriptions into the sort of language that was used in the training brochure. He told me that the company had changed the way that it ordered stationery and his job involved keeping his colleagues happy, informed of any changes, and predicting what stock to carry. We changed this to: analytical forecasting, feedback facilitator and experience in change management. The aim wasn't to hype Kevin's skills, but to show him that he wasn't starting from scratch. For Kevin to be so good at his job he had to have good interpersonal skills, be numerate, good at delegating, efficient at paperwork and much more.

Kevin found the training course a challenge, mainly because of the homework to be done in his own time. He also had to overcome his fear of asking questions when he didn't understand things. However, his confidence grew when he realised that one question from him often opened the floodgates for other trainees to ask questions too. Since qualifying he has had the satisfaction of being told what a valued manager he is and his salary has more than doubled.

Kevin is similar to many people who doubt their own abilities, or have a low level of self-esteem. This may leave you feeling that you can only progress to a certain level before you get 'found out'. It's just as likely to strike the academically proficient as those who believe themselves academically challenged. We all have moments of doubt, and questioning our ability is by no means always a bad thing to do. It becomes a problem when it stops you progressing and getting what you want. In this scenario money isn't evading you – you are evading money because you don't believe in your basic worth.

The world of work is changing so fast you can't afford to rely on any one set of skills keeping you in the job market. Rather than worrying about this, you can focus on the positive opportunities. Qualifications and experience both have value, but that value is doubled when you combine them. And what makes the difference financially is how you apply your skills. What's most in demand right now is being a flexible all-rounder. The modern workplace is a more equal and democratic place, which values a very wide range of skills, and these are achievable by the majority, not just a select few. Money itself is totally non-exclusive; it has no preference where it goes.

▪ Realising Your Worth

What you do with your skills and where you take them makes a huge difference to the income you'll receive. First you must decide where you want to be and the sort of money you want to be earning. You have nothing to lose, and a lot to gain, by getting as much information as possible from companies. When job advertisements offer attractive salaries find out what a company is really looking for. Don't rely on your personal interpretation of what a company means by 'experience'. For example, they may want it in a very specific area and possibly to a level that you haven't yet reached. You can get blinded by the salary at the top of an advert and not see what's actually involved in the job. If you really do have the right skills and experience, believe me you will find a way of realising them.

Sometimes you may get pigeon-holed in a position and bosses fail to see how much you have progressed and the level of responsibility and quality of work you are now capable of. You may have to be brave and tell your boss your real worth. If you don't, you'll simmer with discontent, feeling undervalued and unappreciated. There are some general rules that apply when asking for more money.

How to Ask for More Money

1. Keep in mind what the market will bear in your area and workplace.

2. If you are asking for a salary above the going rate, be sure that you can justify it with the extra returns you will bring the company. Don't think that if you double your output your salary should be doubled. This may not leave the company enough profit, and they won't double your salary if you end up costing them the equivalent in profit.

3. If your company has annual pay reviews this is usually the best time to approach them. If you get an appraisal at this time, wait until you receive this. You won't have a very good case for a pay rise if your appraisal isn't good. If you ask for more money up front, some bosses could deliberately weaken your appraisal to give them more bargaining power and you less.

4. Don't be put off if your request is declined. What you need now is to ensure it won't be declined next time. Be up front and ask what you have to do to increase your income. It could involve learning new skills or taking on additional responsibility. This lets you see what's important to the employer, which isn't always what you think.

5. Don't be tempted to use comparisons, such as a colleague who is on more money for the same job or another

company that pays higher for the same job. These arguments can sound like ultimatums or threats, and you only push your employer to either defend or justify their position.

6. Always appear enthusiastic about your work. Your job description may have changed considerably, and it's OK to highlight what additional responsibility and workloads you have taken on. Emphasise your contribution in a positive way. For example, say, 'When I joined the company I was responsible for controlling the budget on new projects. I have now progressed to a level where I am responsible for overseeing the whole project.' Don't say, 'It's not fair that I have all this additional responsibility and am paid the same rate.' You don't want to come over as only interested in how much money you can make.

Often there is a fine line between an employer wanting to see you giving that bit extra, and them taking advantage of you. Some people knock on their boss's door the minute their workload increases. But, at the other end of the scale there are those who sit back until their workload reaches an unmanageable level and they start to experience real stress. You need to monitor the situation constantly. Be prepared to give your employer feedback about your work and don't relate every conversation to money. Many situations are unfair, but putting your case forward in a negative way can earn you the reputation of being a troublemaker, unwilling to accommodate company needs and only interested in your own gain. Give some thought to the culture of the organisation you work in (see Chapter 4). There is little chance of having your true value realised by a company that is not in the habit of rewarding staff efforts.

▪ Be Proactive

Smart workers don't sit back waiting for an opportunity to fall into their lap; they make themselves available to opportunity. Even when they are headhunted it's no accident. They have either positioned themselves at the top of their profession or in a highly competitive market place where headhunting is a recognised way of finding staff. Being stuck in a job where you feel undervalued, with your CV under wraps, won't get you the recognition you want. The idea of self-marketing doesn't appeal to everyone, but if this is a block for you then it's one you need to work to overcome.

There are so many ways to get information on job opportunities today that there really is no excuse for being left behind. Most newspapers have job and career sections, the Internet advertises jobs and there are private and publicly funded careers advisory services. Networking is also a really good option. Don't ask friends directly to recommend you for a job. This puts them in a difficult position and no one should assume that the boundaries of friendship extend to this area. However, you could ask friends to provide you with the name and address of someone you could send your CV to or request information on an area that you are interested in. A highly paid job can be snapped up without a company even having to advertise, because of people using their initiative in just these ways.

▪ Same Job – Different Salary?

One thing I discovered very quickly as an employer is that when you give a member of staff a salary increase you can almost guarantee a steady flow of requests for salary increases from other staff. They may think they are doing the same job as a colleague, when actually they aren't. For example, I employed an administrator who was so good at her job I significantly increased her salary. When she eventually left the company, several staff members were keen to have the vacancy and the salary that went with it. However, the same salary was not on offer because, in reality, the job now needed two people to do it. I knew what the role involved and the level of skills my previous employee had, and that she had been extraordinary.

Exceptionally skilled individuals can make a role look easy and in the wrong company they can be undervalued. Now I don't want to give the impression that I was employer of the year and good at spotting staff potential. The truth of the matter is that my clever administrator helped me see her worth with some great negotiation.

She quickly got to grips with her role and could see that she was capable of handling much more. This is not something an employer would usually spot. Over time she offered to take on more work and politely asked for me to consider a pay review if I was happy with her progress. Not only was I happy, I felt she was doing me a huge favour. Had my administrator just gone ahead and taken on additional work, I might never have noticed. Worse still I might have taken her work for granted and assumed she was doing no more than expected. An employer can't have the insight that you have into the role you perform. By going ahead and taking on more work you could be making a rod for your own back. As a rule, up-front negotiation is always more profitable.

Let's say you can see a way of producing five times as much work. Why not find out in advance what you could expect to receive for doing this? Hoping your employer will notice anyway is usually hoping for too much – although you can guarantee that if you pull in your reins someone will notice the decline in your productivity. You know your value and the contribution you are capable of making. Don't waste energy wondering why your employers can't see it for themselves. Help them to see your worth and do it in a way that allows you to prosper.

▪ Coaching Review

► There are other values besides financial ones that have to be satisfied by work.

► Take control of your finances before trying to increase your income or you could end up with the same financial worries.

► Regardless of your skills, not all sectors of the workplace offer the same financial rewards – especially when there are fixed pay structures in place.

► Being a multi-skilled and flexible worker is what's most in demand.

► With training and experience you can significantly increase your earning potential.

► When asking for a pay rise make sure you follow the basic rules.

► If you can see a way to take on more work and increase your productivity, negotiate your worth up front.

► Be proactive – if you have skills let people know about them.

CHAPTER EIGHT

I Don't Have a Problem

YOU CAN'T ALWAYS LIKE everyone you work with, but it makes life a lot easier if you can find a way to get on with them. The workplace is a hotbed of human relationships. While the culture of an organisation can certainly influence the behaviour and types of attitudes you come across (see Chapter 4), people are people and you will find the same personality traits wherever you work. Recognising these different traits can be enormously helpful in the way you deal with people, helping you to avoid reacting negatively, taking things personally or becoming caught up in other people's dramas.

Work can provide you with a wonderful sense of community and a feeling of belonging with good, supportive relationships built on strong bonds of trust, respect and goodwill. On the flip side poor relationships are one of the most challenging aspects of working life. They can be emotional triggers, leaving you feeling misunderstood and equally unable to understand where the other person is coming from.

It is not enough for me as a coach to tell you that people are different and the best way forward is to accept this and leave them to get on with it. Not only is that easier said than done, it's not an approach that actually works. Why? Because you are not working in isolation. How other people behave does affect you on both a practical and emotional level. There is merit in tolerance and being able to accept others, but that's not to say you can stay passive and neutral in interactive relationships of which you are part.

▪ Negotiating Work Relationships

Coaching is about dealing with people and situations in a positive way, and one that moves you forward. Relationships do need boundaries and putting those in place is part of the process. The aim is not to change others or find a way of manipulating them to behave to patterns you dictate, after all, that's not how any of us want to be treated. You need to stand back from the emotional blocks that can so easily occur. When people experience a breakdown in a relationship they often convince themselves they are doing everything to rectify the situation. However, if you are reacting to negative emotions such as anger, frustration, fear and possibly a deep-rooted dislike for another person, then you are not doing everything.

A common reaction is the 'I don't have a problem, they do' reaction. But if the relationship you have with your colleagues is not workable, then *you* have a problem.

Of course, some people can be an absolute pain. They have a knack of pushing all the wrong buttons, to such a point that we react physically and our body literally tenses up in their company. I've watched clients relay conversations to me about these kinds of people and their discomfort is evident. Telling them to ignore the other person would certainly not help. They have to stop the situation getting out of hand in the first place. This means knowing your boundaries and how to enforce them. Lisa's story is a classic case of the straw that broke the camel's back.

When Lisa came to see me she was tearful and so fed up with her colleague Elaine that she felt like resigning. She had a long list of complaints against Elaine, but the situation had come to a head over something that seemed small and petty. Lisa had walked into the staff room to find Elaine making a cup of tea – a fairly innocuous action. However, Lisa had blown a fuse, claiming that Elaine never contributed to the tea bag kitty and so had no right to help herself. She proceeded to yell at Elaine in front of the other staff. Her colleagues were all surprised as normally she never lost her temper. Elaine was furious at being yelled at in public, and demanded an apology from Lisa otherwise she would report her for misconduct.

The threat of being reported was Lisa's immediate problem, as it could escalate the situation, but she didn't want to apologise to Elaine as she felt so strongly about her. There was obviously more to the situation.

'OK, she doesn't give to the tea bag kitty. Does that justify your behaviour?' I asked.

'Perhaps my behaviour was out of order, but you don't know what she's like. There's other stuff,' Lisa admitted. Then came a long list of Elaine's faults. Elaine often made intrusive remarks. She often came back late from lunch, delaying Lisa's appointments as she couldn't leave until Elaine returned. She kept talking to Lisa when Lisa was on the phone. The list continued. None of it was major in isolation, but it was a case of the drip, drip, drip effect that can push the best of us over the edge. What became clear as she talked was that Lisa was getting this 'other stuff' off her chest for the first time. She didn't like confrontation and hadn't said a word to anyone until the situation had built up and caused her to explode over a seemingly petty incident.

She knew it all sounded petty in isolation and was embarrassed at what her boss would think. Lisa needed to see that reacting in the wrong way can make the problem worse - which it had. Lisa decided an apology would be the best way to stop things getting out of hand.

But we also worked together on establishing boundaries. It was important for Lisa to see that setting boundaries does not require you to make a fuss, be aggressive or face a confrontation.

Lisa apologised to Elaine and even offered to do so in front of the staff members who had witnessed the scene. Elaine declined this, but the gesture was appreciated. She responded by inviting Lisa for a drink after work and took this opportunity to tell her that she always felt Lisa didn't really like her and she couldn't understand why.

Between them they made a lot of progress that evening and were even able to laugh at the misunderstandings that had arisen. Lisa could see how her behaviour attracted the attention of a colleague who, though irritating, simply wanted to be liked. They didn't become bosom pals, but their new-found understanding led to a healthy and workable relationship.

Making an apology can't have been an easy thing for Lisa to do. Haven't we all had a family member, friend, partner or work associate push us to the edge? Emotion often overrules logic. Even when you know rationally that a difference is insignificant or seems ridiculous, that may not be enough to stop you feeling the way you do. You're going to crash into a wall when you keep running with, 'I can't make anyone understand how I feel', 'Why are they treating me this way?' and 'It's not fair'. Better to convert these sentiments to 'I need to communicate my needs or how I feel as clearly as possible', 'How can I turn this situation around and get the results I want?' and 'This situation is not working for me and I need to find a balanced solution that will keep everyone happy.'

Experiences are unique. No two people have the same ones, or react in the same way. It can take a lifetime of work just understanding the complexities of your own personality, never mind getting to grips with anyone else's. Being willing to try does make a difference. If you know that you've acted irrationally – or overreacted – an apology is a better option. In such situations you can't justify your own behaviour by trying to negate another person's.

For whatever reason there are certain people with whom we are more likely to have misunderstandings. I'm not referring to those who are generally regarded as socially inept, rather the people we meet who just get on our nerves. Outside of work we can usually avoid them. The difference with work is that is throws us together with a whole bunch of personalities. We all need the company of others, but we also need space and territory. This is something easily invaded when you don't have clear boundaries.

▪ Setting Boundaries

Just think about it. *You* have a problem with someone at work, but does everyone else? Just as you may have taken an instant dislike to someone, someone has taken a dislike to you, for no reason you can fathom. You can't be attracted to every personality you meet any more than they can be attracted to you. Ego causes us to judge by our own standards which can put us in an 'I'm right, you're wrong' mentality. But we've all been wrong and made judgements based on lack of information and inaccurate perception of the situation.

Instinct can serve you well, but you may need to stand back from instinct and consider all the information. The starting point is to get your own boundaries in place and relate them to the person you are, before trying to relate to the person you think someone else is.

▪ The Formula for Establishing Your Boundaries

Focus

Think about someone you struggle to get on with. Make a list of the things about the person that annoy you. With every point of irritation use a scoring system from one to ten. Anything above a five means their behaviour is beyond what you find acceptable.

Here are some suggestions to get you started, perhaps they:

- Make tactless remarks   1 2 3 4 5 6 7 8 9 10
- Take liberties   1 2 3 4 5 6 7 8 9 10
- Try to control you   1 2 3 4 5 6 7 8 9 10
- Never listen   1 2 3 4 5 6 7 8 9 10
- Are a bully   1 2 3 4 5 6 7 8 9 10

Think about how anything above a five makes you feel. Bear in mind that the other person may both be unaware of the effect they have on you and not deliberately setting out to cause a problem. You must establish your line of acceptable behaviour and take responsibility for helping other people not to cross it.

Organise

The solution to your problem comes from knowing your boundaries and being able to communicate them. You can do this by organising your thoughts and feelings so that you are aware of things that upset you and the type of behaviour that makes you feel someone has overstepped the mark. What puts a lot of people off is the idea of confrontation, but that can be because they only associate it with unpleasantness. I remind my clients that at times we need to confront our own behaviour and attitudes.

If you can find a way of doing this without beating yourself up and causing negative emotions like guilt and shame, you will have the skills to confront others positively. Keeping your own behaviour in check shows an awareness of the consequences of it. You may feel like giving someone a dressing down, but you don't because you don't want to hurt their feelings. However, saying nothing is not the best option if they are likely to repeat similar behaviour. Instead of having one grievance you will end up with several and reach boiling point like Lisa did. What happens next is overreaction rather than acceptable action. Here are some guidelines for communicating boundaries positively.

- Use a boundary that allows a solution. For example, your boss constantly fails to prioritise the work he gives you, which results in you being reprimanded for not completing urgent tasks. The solution is to ask for a time-frame for completion for every piece of work you are given. Update your boss with what else you are working on so those time-frames can be constantly clarified. Highlighting time emphasises the problem and asking for a time-frame allows your boss to solve the problem by prioritising what's urgent. A boundary with no solution would be you saying you can't take on any more work.

- Refrain from making personal remarks or being critical. Better to say 'Can you take your lunch later as this is our busiest time of day?' than 'How can you be so inconsiderate as to take your lunch at the busiest time of day?'.

- An appropriate compliment can help you establish different ways of working. Team working is productive, but problems can arise because all people have different ways of working. For example, you are good at getting through a large volume of work and someone on your team constantly interrupts you with detail. Point out to them how good their attention to detail is and the relevance of this to the project. At the same time, emphasise your way of working and the need to combine both approaches. You can jointly come up with a way of working that allows you to do what you do best and let your colleague attend to detail without interrupting your flow. Criticising their way of working will only make them defensive and looking for fault with yours.

Review

If you find it difficult to communicate boundaries you have to ask why this is.

► Has it led to confrontation in the past?

► Are you worried about being disliked or coming across as difficult?

► Are you concerned about being misunderstood?

► Are you afraid to address what the real issue is?

► Do you think the other person 'should just know' your boundaries without you having to explain them?

It may be easier to think someone is at fault because they make you feel inadequate, when your real issue could be lack of self-esteem. The truth is that no one can make you feel inadequate without your own consent. To stop patterns repeating requires honesty about the real reason your buttons are being pushed. Deal with the existing situation rather than projecting unresolved past experiences. For instance, a controlling boss could evoke memories of a controlling parent or previous boss, and cause the same old emotional reaction. But they are not the same people and a previous negative experience has no place in a different set of circumstances. Seeing a pattern is the first step to breaking it.

Motivate

Every time you set a boundary you will feel motivated, because not only are you learning to be assertive, you are also helping others to behave in a way that is acceptable to you. Form a positive association with boundaries and see these boundaries as a way of motivating the right behaviour rather than highlighting negative behaviour. In effect you are coaching others to contribute towards good relationships. How you think about yourself will also help your motivation to take action. Do you want to go through life thinking you are the sort of person who will always experience problems because of a head-in-the-sand approach? Or would you prefer to think of yourself as the sort of person who learns from previous mistakes and deals with things before they escalate?

Utilise

What are your strengths? Knowing your boundaries is definitely one. So is not leaving things to chance by letting other people know what those boundaries are. It's down to you to enforce them. Being willing to take responsibility for communicating and enforcing your boundaries is a major strength because so many people sit back and wallow in being the injured party. Now that may sound unfair – after all a breakdown in any relationship can leave you hurt and confused. I understand that, so I'm not being unsympathetic. The point is that negative emotions, left unchallenged, fester and grow. They damage you more than any person. Another person may be subjected to your behaviour and harsh words, but you are constantly subjected to your thoughts and emotions. Making things work for you does require you to be proactive and assertive. This is a worthwhile challenge because it demonstrates that you respect your own needs and boundaries, which is an essential strength if you want other people to respect them.

Liberate

Don't limit the outcome of a relationship. The majority of misunderstandings are easily avoided through effective dialogue. You may make an inaccurate judgement when you don't have all the facts, just as another person may do about you. Remember

Lisa and Elaine? Elaine was trying to be liked and get to know Lisa better. Lisa found Elaine's behaviour annoying and intrusive. Neither set out to be malicious or vindictive. Don't let hurt pride or feelings stand in the way of connecting with another person. Pulling back is defensive and not always necessary. Liberate yourself with some new questions, such as 'What's to stop me making the first move?', 'Have I been clear about what the problem is?', 'Are my beliefs based on real evidence or assumptions?', 'Have I any reason or evidence to believe this person deliberately set out to cause me a problem?'.

If someone's behaviour really is outside the lines of acceptability – bullying, sexual harassment, racism – don't limit the outcome by believing there is nothing you can do. Legal and tribunal proceedings are there to protect your rights. You also have your internal protection mechanism, which signals to you when your line has been crossed.

Act

Progress comes from taking positive action, but it can also provoke resistance. If, for example, taking long lunches became an established practice in a company, no longer being allowed to do so would feel like an inconvenience. Breaking bad habits provokes protest. Emotions are childlike and they often defy logic. Just as a child will scream and protest at the protective action of a parent, we as adults have our own tantrums. There's that little voice in our head saying 'Why should I be nice to someone I don't like?', 'Why should I have this extra workload?', 'Why should I be the one to make the first move?'.

The problem with 'why' questions is that you soon run out of answers. Concentrate on taking action to stop, improve, prevent and move forward. This begins with solution-oriented questions that begin with how, rather than why. For example, 'How can I make it work for me?', 'How can I turn things around?', 'How can I demonstrate the way I feel?'.

Once again, you are now ready to 'face' the challenge (see page 10). By making the necessary changes you will experience the right results.

▪ How Well Do You Know People?

It's fun to indulge in a bit of armchair psychology, trying to figure out why people behave the way they do. But these assessments are based on speculation and can actually be very inaccurate. A work colleague could think you are a control freak, when you perceive you are just trying to make sure things get done properly. Equally, you could be judged as indecisive when you are the sort of person who doesn't like to make hasty decisions.

Of course, it's impossible not to form opinions about people. And let's not forget that we also form lots of positive one. We think of people as being charming, considerate, easy to get along with, good fun. I know lots of staff who may be wary of a strict boss with high standards, but respect them and have no problem working with them. Individual human behaviour has a broad spectrum and, overall, if we have good social skills, our level of tolerance and flexibility is good. Everyone experiences bad days and moods and the effects are two-way. It's not much fun being around an irritable colleague, but chances are they have been on the receiving end of your mood at some point.

A certain amount of confrontation, difference of opinion and personality clash is to be expected. The effects should not be long lasting or damaging. Regular confrontation, however, is a problem. When clients come to see me because they are experiencing it, eight times out of ten they tell me they have the worst boss/manager/partner/colleague. Maybe you feel this way too. But the disadvantage is that if you continue with this line of thought you will remain blocked. You also need to think about any ways in which *your* behaviour could be affecting the situation. Of course, you don't make your problem colleague a bully, control freak or give them any other unpleasant character trait. That's down to them. But inadvertently you may be behaving in a way that either attracts them to you or provides the dynamics that bring out undesirable behaviour.

The list that follows is not designed to fit people into rigid categories. What it does is take the most difficult character traits you may come across and show you how to deal with them.

1. The Controller

Without doubt this is the most commonly used term I hear, especially when describing a boss. If a person has a controlling nature you can be sure that a position of authority would highlight this. The controller has an obsession with controlling not only themselves, but also those around them. Their sense of drive often leads to them holding senior positions. Being in charge requires a level of control, and controllers can make very good bosses. But, at their worst, they can be absolute nightmare bosses who find it difficult to delegate power and have to have the final say on every issue. The worst sort of controller you can encounter is one that undermines and criticises you.

How to deal with the controller

► Be careful not to allow yourself to be set up. Agreeing to take on too much work, not being properly briefed or given specific time-frames for work, and reacting defensively all give the controller a free run. After the event they have a knack of deflecting blame back to you.

► Know your boundaries and stay solution oriented. Don't try telling a controller you can't work late that evening because you have other commitments. Their agenda will always take priority over yours. Look to see if you can give them an alternative. Perhaps a colleague will swap with you, you can come in early the next morning or work late the next evening. I'm not suggesting you fall over backwards to accommodate their every whim. Just do not create an association in their mind that you are a problem, because that's exactly the sort of person controllers target. To give them a problem is to resist their control and they will use their power to override you. Give them a solution, which also suits you and diffuses the dynamics.

► Stay focused. Controllers are good at causing chaos. They can have you running all over the place as they constantly move the goalposts. In order to cope, take the stance of a tennis player moving from one foot to the other to cover what direction the ball is coming from. The problem is that you are now focusing on their agenda and waiting for direction, afraid to make a move in case you get it wrong. Rather than wait for direction, seek direction. If you have a specific job to do, clarify up front what the objectives are and what areas you are to take responsibility for. Try and establish at what stage you are expected to report back to them or give them an update.

► Help them to trust your ability. Controllers often mistrust the ability of staff and they are not good at encouraging them to use their initiative. Keep the lines of communication open and tell them what areas you are confident to handle in advance so that you can reach an agreement. A critical controller finds fault when they don't feel involved. Their involvement can be an irritation, but you can gradually gain their trust and expand on the areas you can take responsibility for. Over time their interference will become less. See the problem as their inability to trust and work towards solving that, rather than the problem being them questioning your ability, because this will make you feel resentful and undermined.

2. The Opposer

You know the sort – they always have an objection. From the smallest decision to the biggest they are quick to point out why it's a bad idea. The opposer does not demonstrate leadership qualities and is more comfortable in a position that allows them to review or focus their attention on other people's work. Always quick to present a problem, opposers don't follow through with a solution.

How to deal with the opposer

► Don't waste time and energy justifying or defending yourself, opposers are not open to ideas or change. State your case with confidence and conviction, and show you are not seeking their support by acting on it.

► Ask them for some alternative suggestions, which is one of the fastest ways to silence them.

► Don't take their comments personally: this is not a reflection of your ability, it's a reflection of their behaviour pattern. Observe and you will see them behaving the same way with others.

► Extend some level of tolerance, as they may well be so fearful of change that they habitually resist it.

3. The Chameleon

The only thing that is predictable about the chameleon is their unpredictability. You just never know who you are dealing with from one day to the next. They are not the sort of person you can count on for support because they change their mind as often as their mood. They don't demonstrate qualities of loyalty and will easily adapt to whatever suits them best. The chameleon is an expert at disappearing into the background at the first sign of trouble and will happily leave you carrying the can.

How to deal with the chameleon

► Don't try to force chameleons to take a stand on any issue. They are fence sitters and even when you think you have their agreement they are likely to go back on anything they say. Before giving your opinion ask them for their opinion. Chances are they won't be forthcoming, but at least you will know the state of play.

► Don't confide in them anything you wish to remain confidential. Relay information that is factual or related to company policy and keep personal remarks out of the conversation. Better to say, 'The department has been requested to work an hour's overtime today', than 'I'm not happy at working an hour's overtime today.'

► Make sure you stay consistent and are not trying to work to their agenda. When you say you are going to do something, make sure you do.

► Don't waste time trying to figure them out or predict what they will do next.

4. The Bully

Unfortunately we don't leave bullies behind in the playground. They are the most unpleasant personalities to encounter at work, especially when in a position of authority. I've coached clients whose lives have been made a misery by bullies, their confidence and self-esteem shattered by the daily onslaught. This is not a character trait I am going to dress up because left unchallenged bullies don't curb or monitor their behaviour. You can't make it your duty to change their behaviour, but you can make it your responsibility to change how they behave towards you as Christine did in Chapter 1. Remember, initially she focused on how badly her boss behaved, but when she took responsibility for changing her own behaviour and reactions she was able to find a solution.

How to deal with the bully

- ► Firstly recognise that bullies don't bully everyone. So it helps to look at the sort of people they don't bully and identify what they may be doing differently to you. Are they more assertive? Do they react differently? Have they got clear boundaries?

- ► Don't think like a victim (thinking you are powerless), behave like a victim (being defensive, fearful and emotional) or act like a victim (acting helpless and not asserting yourself). You can do something and you can change your behaviour. You can take action by finding out what your rights are. You have legal rights and your contract of employment may cover terms for grievances and complaints.

- ► Communicate your boundaries. The bully is thick skinned and even the word 'No' may have to be reinforced. The best way to reinforce any statement is through your actions. So, if you have said no to doing something, don't go ahead and do it and think that because you have moaned about it in the process you will get your message across. All this does is show the bully they can manipulate you and force you to do something you don't want to do.

▪ Are You the Enemy?

We all like to think we're the good guys. But we can't all be good all the time. It's only through questioning your own behaviour that you can really improve it. How often do you hear people describe themselves as aggressive, troublemakers, bullies, difficult, inconsiderate to other people's feelings? Not often I suspect. And they are certainly not descriptions we could easily apply to ourselves. But there are some warning signs that indicate all is not well, including:

▶ constant confrontation, arguments, misunderstandings

▶ losing your temper easily

▶ raising your voice

▶ having people clam up around you, unable to confide in you or open up to you.

Another sign of a problem is receiving regular criticism from several sources. Criticism is often a defence mechanism against attack and if you are getting more than your fair share you have to question why.

How we see ourselves does not always align with how others see us. I've heard lots of comments along these lines, 'I can't believe my staff are afraid of me, I'm a real softy', 'I can't believe he thinks I'm aggressive, he's the aggressive one', 'I'm not a bully, I just have to show them who's boss around here.' We can all do a great job justifying our behaviour and reflecting it in a positive light. That's fine if other people agree with us. But if relationships break down on a regular basis we need to stop denying reality. All relationships have to be worked at including the ones we treasure most.

▪ Reinforcing Good Relationships

EXERCISE

The following exercise will help you to identify ways to reinforce good relationships.

1. Make a list in your journal of at least three people you really like who are either friends or work colleagues. Leave out partners and family because in very close relationships we can overlook both good and bad qualities, and find it more difficult to be objective.

2. Next to each person you have listed, make a list of their positive qualities, for example 'They are a good listener, supportive, have a sense of humour, can be trusted, are generous, considerate . . .'

3. With each quality you list spend a few minutes thinking about how each person demonstrates it. So, for example, if you like someone because they are supportive how have they supported you? Have they encouraged or praised your performance? Did they offer words of comfort when you had a problem? Did they help you master a skill?

4. Now make a list of your own personal qualities and next to each one write a few sentences on how you put these qualities into action:

QUALITY	ACTION
I am very loyal to my company	I always speak highly of the company I never reveal confidential information
I am very considerate to others	I ask people for their feedback and opinion I enjoy sharing my skills and knowledge I make time to listen to problems

The purpose of this is to get you focused on what qualities contribute to forming good relationships and let you see if you are actually reflecting those qualities in your own behaviour. What you need to look for is evidence.

Here are some other ways to see how good you are at forming relationships:

- If you are a good communicator – you won't experience regular misunderstandings or confrontation.

- If you are a good listener – people will find it easy to open up to you.

- If you are supportive – people will come to you when they have a problem.

- If you are trustworthy – people will be quick to confide sensitive and confidential information with you.

- If you have a professional approach to work – others are unlikely to cut corners or perform badly around you.

In my experience very few people deliberately set out to offend, alienate, upset or cause confrontation. While their behaviour may be inappropriate, their intentions are often good. Unfortunately, that's not enough because the perception and judgements others make about you are based on your behaviour.

▪ Coaching Review

▶ Know your boundaries and take responsibility for communicating them.

▶ Your boundary marks your line of acceptability. Respect the fact that other people also have boundaries.

▶ Don't make judgements based on assumptions. The majority of misunderstandings can be cleared up by dialogue and getting more information.

▶ It takes two people to have a breakdown in a relationship, so you have to take responsibility for your own actions and behaviour.

▶ You can only have good relationships when you relate to people in a positive way.

▶ Be careful how you think about others and describe them. Are you prone to finding fault? Are you quick to criticise? Are you dismissive? You need to counteract this by focusing on positive traits not highlighting negative ones.

▶ Monitor your own reactions and behaviour, and make sure you are not guilty of repeating all the traits you dislike.

► Good relationships are fundamental to your happiness and you have to make a commitment to achieving them.

► Set yourself positive goals for relationships. Good ones include: I'm going to give more positive feedback; I'm going to take the time to work at this relationship; I'm going to overlook past issues and make a fresh start. Set down your specific goals in your journal.

CHAPTER NINE

Power Struggles

I N CHAPTER 8 WE discussed relationships at work, and the useful techniques for improving them and dealing with the people around you. In some ways, this chapter is about the same subject but taken to a new level, because it deals with power struggles, office politics and competitiveness. You really need to understand how they operate if you want to succeed at work. Why? Because research shows that 75 per cent of people who fail in their jobs do so because of political problems, not skill deficiencies. Office politics exist in all workplaces and – as with all politics – they are about getting power, using it and misusing it.

Wouldn't it be great if only the good guys got to the top? But in the real world it's not only cream that rises to the top, but grease as well! Of course, you can choose to ignore who really holds the power in the workplace if you don't like them much, but you do so at your own peril. The bottom line is that these people can significantly affect how well you progress in your organisation. I'm not saying it should, or that it is right – just that it does. So in this chapter I'm going to get down to the nitty gritty and reveal how things really do work, rather than how things should work, and then help you deal with that reality on your own terms.

People coming into the workplace for the first time usually have little if any knowledge of office politics, and that's because it is rarely discussed – at least not in any obvious way. You won't see a job description stating you have to be skilled in office politics anywhere. Instead, it's often dressed up at job interviews when you are told the importance of fitting into the team, sharing objectives, sharing the company philosophy and culture. As well as getting to grips with a job, you have to manoeuvre your way round any potential landmines. And unless you figure out where they're placed you will go through your career stepping on them.

By understanding power struggles, office politics and aggressive competition you can steer clear of those landmines. This chapter isn't about copying some of the negative behaviour and attitudes we'll be discussing, but about how to use it to your advantage and not becoming the victim of it. There is more than one way to get ahead at work and the route you choose will be determined by your values and the sort of person you are.

▪ Are You a Smart Worker?

Have you ever wondered why some people work really hard, never step out of line and yet fail to get ahead at work? And then there are those who don't seem to over-stretch themselves, yet get recognition and reward for everything they do. They're the 'smart' workers – the ones who know how to work the system. They know who holds the power and – equally important – who has influence. Having influence won't necessarily come from rank. The MD's secretary may not hold the rank but they can have a huge amount of influence. Knowledge is also essential to the smart worker and you can guarantee they take advantage of the grapevine. You may not enjoy the gossip element of the grapevine, but it does pay to keep your ear to the ground if you want to know what is really going on and how the culture of an organisation works at its roots.

Being a smart worker is one of the most useful skills you can possibly have. Just like those soft, interpersonal skills that were discussed in Chapter 1, it's not something that is directly teachable like a hard core skill.

To explain the difference, let's say I was teaching you a hard core skill such as motor mechanics. The theoretical side would require you to have a certain level of intelligence to understand, retain and repeat the information. The practical side would come with repetition and experience of doing the job. Most of us don't experience too much of a problem learning hard core skills, although we will certainly find some things naturally easier than others. Soft and interpersonal skills are very different because there is not a set 'correct' theory to follow. They are emotionally, personality and value based. They involve very personal qualities like integrity, honesty, your level of self-worth, how you deal with responsibility and how you form relationships. The practical side of interpersonal skills covers equally hard to pin down elements, like body language and the signals you give off. Because they are so intangible, and harder to define, some people not only get this wrong, but are left feeling confused and frustrated because they have no idea why they got it wrong.

That's not to say you can't learn soft skills or how to be a smart worker – you definitely can. In the same way as there's no set 'theory' for interpersonal skills, there's no set 'theory' for being a smart worker. That's because the rules are different in every organisation. What's acceptable in one workplace won't be in another. You have to observe what is going on in your workplace. Rather than make judgements based on your own standards, you have to identify the subtle and unspoken standards that actually operate where you work. Here are seven rules you can use to do this and become a smart worker.

The Seven Rules of Being a Smart Worker

These rules are designed to give you the necessary skills to handle office politics and be aware of what leads to power struggles and aggressively competitive behaviour. Office politics can be used to your advantage, so if getting ahead, being promoted and gaining recognition is what you want, learn to work with the system, not against it.

1. You are responsible for your own behaviour

You are responsible for your own behaviour and if people are reacting to you in a negative way you are behaving in a negative way.

Most of us are very aware when work colleagues behave in a difficult way, but we rarely spot our own negative behaviour patterns, which is why we commonly feel baffled when we don't get the reaction we expect.

Good interpersonal skills help us to monitor and – where necessary – modify our own behaviour. People with relatively poor interpersonal skills tend to act on their first emotional impulses, and these will often be the negative ones: anger, fear, frustration, resentment. There are consequences to acting on these emotions. For example, fear of doing a job badly could result in you refusing to do it or leaving it for someone else to do – this could easily be perceived by your work colleagues as being difficult or lazy.

With good interpersonal skills, even if you initially experience a negative reaction to a situation at work, you can regulate your response and act with understanding, tolerance, forgiveness and motivation to handle the situation in a positive way. This inevitably gets much better results.

You may think that acting the way you feel, or going with your instant reactions, is more 'true' to your personality, but the fact is that if this doesn't lead you to getting what you want, you need to adjust the way you react and behave.

2. Play to the professional agenda

If you want to win a power struggle, play to the professional agenda not the personal one.

Winning a power struggle is not determined by what is fair or necessarily right. That's the harsh reality. Those individuals who consistently win power struggles play to a professional agenda not a personal one. This means that they know and understand what really matters in their organisation and reflect this in their strategies.

So, for example, let's say you get caught up in a power struggle with a colleague who takes lengthy lunch breaks. You complain to management, but what you didn't know was that your colleague was using this time to wine and dine powerful clients. Your colleague may hold the same rank as you, but by currying favour with a major client has gained influence over that client that has impressed your boss. Now your colleague still has their personal agenda but they have made a professional advance – it may not be a pleasant one. However, in the eyes of management it may be more valuable than the hours you spent working in the office. So if you want to win you have to know what counts *the most*. Here are a few tips on the sort of things that are generally regarded as significant.

- ▶ **Results** While effort is undoubtedly recognised more by some organisations than others, it's results that consistently get rewarded.

- ▶ **Speed** This is the ability to get a job done fast.

- ▶ **Being able to predict or counteract any threat from competition** To do this you have to keep up with market forces and know what is going on your industry. Be proactive, make suggestions, offer solutions, plan ahead and be prepared to say what you think in advance. Reactive staff always wait for the post-mortem, but don't expect credit for knowledge gained or given in hindsight.

- ▶ **Always look at the bigger picture** This is basically a company's overall objective. Don't get bogged down with detail, because this will pull you into a personal agenda. Think of your employer as sitting in their car and trying to get from A to B. The smart worker always keeps the engine running. The worker who gets bogged down in detail tries to tell their employer how their part of the engine works.

3. Help others get what they want

You will only consistently get what you want by helping others get what they want.

You are not working in isolation and getting what you want only happens when others co-operate. At work those in authority can use coercive behaviour to get what they want, but it doesn't work in the long run. Enforced co-operation – given grudgingly and therefore likely to be withdrawn as soon as possible – is nowhere near as good as voluntary co-operation – given willingly in a win-win situation. When you are giving other people what they want they not only give extra in return, but you can also gain their trust, loyalty and respect. For example, if you have a specialist skill and teach it to a colleague, they will benefit from this additional skill and you could get recognition in the process for being a team player and increasing the potential of another worker.

4. Respect the pecking order

Respect the pecking order within a company. You may doubt the ability of a superior but, remember, someone higher probably doesn't.

Even in informal workplaces a certain pecking order exists and unless you respect this you will experience the undesirable side of office politics. Colleagues may not share the opinion you have of a superior. Think very carefully before ever going over a superior's head. You may not be breaching company regulations, but you could be breaching the accepted code of conduct. So, always deal with the person you are expected to in the first instance and aim to keep the lines of communication positive. If you have a complaint or grievance refer to Chapter 6 and the section entitled 'The Effective Negotiator'. This discusses the importance of putting your case forward without making the other person wrong.

If you have exhausted all possibilities and really believe it is necessary to go above a superior's head, stick to objective facts, and avoid personal and emotive arguments. Better to say, 'I have a misunderstanding with my manager over deadlines I'm having a problem resolving' than ' It's impossible to work for my manager because he is incapable is setting realistic deadlines.' The person above your superior may have appointed your superior and therefore the second statement questions the ability of both parties.

5. Recognise who has the power

Recognise who has the power and influence. It doesn't pay to upset the wrong people.

There are some people it really is not wise to cross swords with. I'm not suggesting you have to become a 'yes' person, simply that there are consequences for upsetting someone who has influence and power, because their opinion of you will affect the treatment you receive from them and others. Colleagues may moan about them and question their decisions and policies behind their back, but watch carefully. They draw the line at any direct confrontation. Even if you have colleagues who quietly support you, don't expect to get it publicly. For whatever reason, those with influence have gained a status and can rely on loyalty from people higher up the ranks. The smart worker gets a good job, then makes sure they keep it. If they want to make waves they always ensure their boat is firmly anchored first in terms of their own position with the company.

6. Don't underestimate what people expect of you

Don't underestimate what people expect of you from their rank.

Do you work the hardest and longest hours in your office and still get no recognition? That's a reality for lots of individuals and leads to frustration and resentment. So what's the answer when you are already giving so much? Well it's to give something different. It's not about how hard you work in the office but how you work the office that counts.

A friend of mine who works for a national newspaper relayed a story to me about a journalist who had worked there for years. Every day he was at his desk working away. Finally he resigned and was complaining to colleagues that after all the years he had worked there the editor never acknowledged him and probably had no idea what he looked like. This got back to the editor and on the day the journalist was clearing his desk the editor walked up, pretended he thought he was the new replacement, shook his hand and welcomed him to the company. Yes – I flinched when I heard the story as well. But there was a powerful message in the editor's snub. According to my friend, lots of the other journalists didn't wait for this admittedly arrogant but busy man to recognise them. Instead, they made themselves know to him, introducing themselves, volunteering for certain jobs, passing on pieces of news or information they thought he would find useful. These were the staff for whom he was accessible and appreciative.

Making yourself known to a boss is important. Don't sit back waiting for people to be impressed by you. Make an impression instantly by making a move in the right direction. Your boss wants to know that you care about what's important to the boss and the relationship you have with them. You have to demonstrate:

▶ **enthusiasm** volunteer for jobs, or sacrifice the occasional lunch hour to finish a job quickly or to sit on committees or working parties

▶ **motivation** come up with your own ideas, anticipating problems rather than just waiting to be told to respond to them

▶ **loyalty** don't gossip about your boss or relay any information given to you in confidence

▶ **commitment** if you say you will do something, take responsibility for doing it directly.

These relationships are crucial to your success. How many bosses do you think sit behind their desk contemplating what they can do to impress you and earn your respect? Not many! That's not to say inconsiderate bosses dominate the workplace. Having the respect of staff is a priority for most managers. However, holding the rank of boss establishes their position and it's your responsibility to confirm your own position.

7. Employers love solutions

Employers love solutions not problems. Doors open when you offer a solution. They slam in your face when all you present is a problem.

We're all good at spotting problems at work – in fact we're too good! Of course, staff having a moan about the management is all part of office politics. It's not the done thing in some workplaces to be singing the praises of the people in charge. Having the right to disagree establishes that you have an opinion and are not just subservient drones. However, the mistake many workers make is to see presenting problems as the only way of maintaining some control over their working lives. They get locked into this mindset and use it to protect their rights.

But don't overlook human nature. None of us actually find it easy to be presented with a problem from someone else. We tend to take it personally and feel criticised. And if you are the person who keeps presenting the problem you become the problem. People see you as negative, critical, objectionable and, ultimately, not on their side. Regardless of how valuable a contribution and how hard working you may be, you will be judged harshly for adopting this mindset and it's also in your interest not to. Why tell someone what you don't want when you can tell them what you do want? When you offer a solution people see you as being helpful, forward thinking, supportive and, perhaps most importantly, on their side.

Henry, the MD of an interior design company, contacted me because he couldn't figure out why he kept having problems with Adam, one of his senior designers. 'Every time he makes a complaint I step in to put things right and he accuses me of undermining him.'

Adam had complained about clients calling him on his mobile at the weekend, so Henry told clients that any calls over the weekend should come through to him. Adam was furious. How could he gain the trust of the client if Henry kept interfering? Then Adam complained that one of the fabric suppliers was extremely rude to him. Henry told the supplier he would use another company unless they changed their attitude to Adam. Adam hit the roof. 'You made me look a complete idiot. Now every time I call the company they are overly nice to me – in fact they are downright patronising.'

I spoke to Adam. He had a list of complaints and grievances ready to read out. I didn't want our conversation to turn into a catalogue of complaints without solutions, so with the first complaint about clients calling him at weekends, I stopped him and asked what would be the alternative. 'Well they can call me at weekends if it's an emergency.' 'So why not tell clients that they can only call you with an emergency at weekends?' I asked. 'Because I need Henry to give me the authority to do that,' Adam replied. The issue of authority came up with the next complaint about the rude supplier. If Adam were in a position to choose or change supplier he would command more respect.

Back to Henry. He had no problem giving Adam more authority once he knew that was what he wanted. Henry need to be coached on asking staff what they wanted when they presented a problem instead of guessing the solution and Adam needed coaching on communicating what he wanted. I got some great feedback from both of them after the session. Apart from their much improved relationship Henry told me that it was a huge relief not to constantly be under pressure to put things right. Adam told me that being given more authority made him feel respected by his boss and able to control problems.

Unless you offer a solution you could end up being given one that makes the problem worse. Henry's intention wasn't to undermine Adam, but when you leave it to someone else to come up with a solution they can't always see the problem from your point of view and their solution, however well meaning, may not be appropriate.

▪ Competitiveness

You can't keep competitiveness out of the workplace because the very nature of business is to be competitive. Companies are competing for customers, profit, additional resources and for good staff. The latter is good news for you. They need the right staff to stay ahead and those with that competitive edge are in big demand. Within an organisation there is also a lot of positive competition and creating incentives to improve performances can motivate staff, increase their sense of purpose, fulfilment and bring financial rewards.

The unpleasant side-effect of all this can be a dog-eat-dog environment. There are more people trying to manoeuvre their way to the top than there are positions available, which leads to aggressive competition, using methods that deliberately sabotage, undermine and attack the performance of others. Not all ambitious people who are completely focused on getting ahead do so by putting co-workers down in the process. There are those who play fair and those who don't. Both types can achieve influence, power and status.

Office politics come about from competition – competing to keep what you have got, get promotion, win power, have influence, stay in favour, make more money, have more choices, be liked and socially accepted as part of the group. When you think about all the things you want from work like recognition, reward, achievement, challenge, success, opportunities to be creative, develop and grow – they are the things that require you to compete because you are not the only one who wants them. Getting what you want is important to you and as you have values they obviously influence what you are prepared to do to get it. This is a good time to consider what those values are and to see if the way you react in competitive situations aligns with them. This is where double standards really expose themselves. If you valued loyalty, having a work colleague gossiping about you would undoubtedly be upsetting. And of course you wouldn't dream of gossiping about them. Or would you?

EXERCISE

Consider the following scenario. Your company has recently announced that it is downsizing. Several jobs are under threat, including your own. A previously friendly workplace is now full of back biting, rumours and gossip. The management makes it known that it will keep all the staff who can demonstrate loyalty to the company. You hear through the grapevine that a colleague is filtering information through to a competitor. Would you report this to management? Pass on the gossip? Ignore it? Make further investigations? Tackle your colleague?

The 'right' answer depends on your values, but that doesn't mean that you would behave in the 'right' way. When jobs are on the line values become like shifting sand and what you assume you will do in theory is not always what you do in practice. Self-preservation often takes top priority in highly competitive situations. No one really knows exactly how they will react until they are put to the test.

Does it make you weak if you readily change your values the minute the stakes get high? No – it only makes you human. You have to deal with the consequences of your own behaviour and it's not for me to tell you what is the right answer, but rather point out that if values are constantly changed for personal convenience, you haven't identified a real value. Competition makes many people deeply uncomfortable because, along with not liking the behaviour it induces in others, they have to deal with the behaviour and reactions it provokes in themselves. You can't avoid it so here are some techniques for dealing with it.

► Review your values (see Chapter 2) and think about how they may be put to the test in competitive situations.

► Don't forget what your goals and objectives are. Be sure you are competing for something you really want.

► Don't use methods to compete that you would object to being used on yourself.

► Don't assume anything ever stays a secret in very competitive workplaces. Only relay what you know is safe to circulate.

► Don't ignore what is and isn't acceptable, otherwise you could use a tactic that results in you being ostracised. Equally, you could fail to demonstrate the competitive edge your employer wants.

► Do take a stand on issues you feel strongly about. You may feel nervous about rocking the boat, but remember if you say nothing it is much more difficult to present your case or have a decision overturned once it has been made.

► Do remain professional at all times. This means remaining loyal to the company if you are intent on staying there. Emotions run high when your position in a company feels threatened, but remember that when things settle down, as they invariably do, you will find it difficult to defend any action taken that damages either the reputation or objectives of a company.

► Do remember that people around you are reacting to how a crisis is affecting them rather than orchestrating a personal campaign against you.

▪ Right Job Wrong Direction?

You love your job and are working with a great team, so what could possibly go wrong? Well, if you overlook who you are accountable to your energies could be pulled in the wrong direction. Giving your best involves applying hard core skills *and* soft ones. It also means applying them in the right direction and satisfying the expectations of the right people. Here are a few examples.

▶ Your boss asks you to prepare new customer order forms. While you're doing this, some of the staff in the office complain how difficult the existing forms are to process. Taking this on board you come up with a much simpler method. Instead of your boss being impressed he wants to know why you didn't follow through and make the form easier for the customer to fill in as well.

▶ You're part of a team working on the development and marketing of a new product. It's your responsibility to write up the report with all the costings. The team doesn't have all the information in time for the deadline, and you don't want to make them look bad, so you stay late preparing an immaculately presented report with colourful graphs, pie charts and elaborate graphics. Your boss is not impressed and wants to know why you are wasting time preparing a report that lacks content.

How would the smart worker have handled these scenarios?

In the first example the smart worker would have known that while work colleagues would appreciate his efforts, making the form easier for customers as well would impress his boss.

In the second example the smart worker would know that preparing a report that lacked content was not meeting the brief and creating work to cover up for missing work would not only leave a boss unimpressed – they could also view it as an insult to their intelligence. The smart worker would let their boss know that they do not have the necessary information to complete the report.

The smart worker likes to keep everyone happy, but ultimately they never forget who they are accountable to and direct their efforts into delivering what is expected of them.

▪ Using the Formula to Improve Your Own Position

Focus

How do power struggles, office politics and competitiveness affect you? List in your journal any specific problems you need to tackle such as being in a power struggle, not understanding the politics or feeling unhappy about what you would have to do to fit in. Also, focus on what you want to achieve and with every problem you identify convert the problem into a goal so you have a positive outcome to focus on. Here are some examples to get you started.

PROBLEM	GOAL
I don't have a good relationship with my boss	Improve my relationship with my boss
I don't think I'm good enough to make it	Improve my confidence skills
High level of competition for promotion	Get promotion

Organise

Make a list of possible solutions. The key to finding a solution in this area is to keep it professional. Things do get personal and you may be up against underhand techniques, but that doesn't mean you have to repeat them. Go over rule 2 of 'How to be a smart worker' (page 161) if power struggles are your problem. If you don't understand how your colleagues operate and feel out on a limb, watch how others interact around you, pay attention to the grapevine, identify who has power and influence by watching to whom colleagues give the most respect. If you really don't like what you would have to do to fit in, give some thought to whether your needs would be best met elsewhere.

Review

If you are constantly running into problems in this area, you are repeating the same mistakes. Remember, don't judge the situation simply by your own standards or by what was acceptable in a previous job. Take stock of your immediate situation and find out what is acceptable there.

Motivate

We are not all motivated by the same things so it helps to identify the things that do motivate you, such as a higher pay cheque, recognition, trust, respect, promotion, responsibility. Doing this will show you what direction to steer your energies in. Even within the same organisation the politics are different at different ranks. The atmosphere may be a lot more relaxed with front-line workers than it is with middle and senior management. For example, if you are motivated by recognition you could receive that for doing your job well as a front-line worker. But higher up the ladder you may be required to do your job well and increase the performance of other staff in order to get recognition. If this is not a responsibility you'd enjoy you won't feel motivated. Therefore, it's important to know exactly what is expected of you so you don't end up doing a job that doesn't provide the motivation you need.

Utilise

Using and developing your interpersonal skills gives you the right resources to handle office politics and resulting power struggles. They definitely give you an advantage, as will being a smart worker. However brilliant you are at your job, you still want to have skills that allow you to form the right relationships.

Liberate

The best way to know if you have any beliefs that are holding you back is to ask yourself 'Am I getting what I want from work?'. If the answer is 'No', then clearly you do have limiting beliefs. Here is a list of some very common beliefs that can hold you back and what you can do to challenge them.

- Believing there is no way to figure out the hidden agenda of office politics. If other people can there is no reason why you can't. You may just need to look harder, give yourself more time to understand the culture or communicate better with your colleagues.

- Believing you are too nice a person to be accepted by colleagues. It's far more likely that colleagues misunderstand you. The workplace can seem like a jungle, but it's not all-out warfare and there is always room for the good guys and peacemakers.

- Believing power only comes from holding a senior rank. This one needs to be narrowed down a bit. You may not have the power to take on senior management or the MD, but power is usually gained in stages, which means first gaining influence at your current level. There are receptionists, secretaries and cleaners who have direct access and influence on the power holders in a company, and they have earned that channel of communication over time without changing their rank.

Act

Unlike in the other chapters of this, I suggest you take time to digest the contents of this chapter before taking action. Not that anything in life is ever black and white, but this area definitely has a bigger grey section. So, it's OK to take more time to get a broader perspective on your own situation. Make a list in your journal of the sort of changes you want to make to improve your position, like improving soft skills, making an impression on the right people, being more/less competitive, becoming a smart worker. Give yourself a deadline for when you will do this.

▪ Facing the Challenge

When you feel ready to take action it's time to 'face' the challenge. There is no definitive rule about when is the right time, but you are in a much better position to do so when your actions are based on the following:

- ▶ being informed, which means getting as much information as possible about a situation before you act

► knowing what you want to achieve, which means listing your goals

► acting on your values, which means knowing what they are and making a commitment to living by them

► seeing the bigger picture, which in this context means asking yourself if your life (not just your working life) will benefit from the actions you take.

▪ Coaching Review

► Around 75 per cent of people who fail in their jobs do so because of political problems, not skill deficiencies.

► Office politics exist in all workplaces.

► It pays to listen to the grapevine.

► Use the seven rules and learn how to be a smart worker.

► You need to know who has the power and the influence.

► Employers expect you to make an effort to impress them.

► If you want to win a power struggle, you have to know what counts most to an organisation and play to its professional agenda, not your own personal one.

► Always remember who you are accountable to because their opinion of you matters.

► It doesn't pay to upset the wrong people.

► Good interpersonal skills are as essential as hard core skills.

► All workplaces are competitive.

► Use your values to make the right decision.

► To survive office politics you have to know what is expected of you on every level.

CHAPTER TEN

Technological Overload and Stress

MUCH OF THIS BOOK has focused on dealing with people, with work and with the different circumstances and situations that human relationships create. But, of course, it's not just office relationships that you have to deal with in the modern workplace. New technology and the changing world of work are also having a huge effect.

Just a few short years ago, we were all looking forward to the technology promise. Technology would make our lives easier, reduce our working hours and the only thing we'd have to worry about was what to do with all that extra free time. Another debunked theory! Instead, working hours have increased, 40 per cent of absenteeism is stress related, work intensification is becoming the norm and we are seeing the new breed of info-slave fast on their way to burnout. Via the Internet, e-mail, voice mail and ubiquitous mobiles, technology has become the thief of time.

One reason that the technology promise didn't deliver was a basic corporate rule we all overlooked: find a way to do something in half the time and you can do twice as much. That's the reality for many and the odds keep getting higher in a competitive global market place. The problem isn't only work related. We have bought into the technology boom in a big way. We are turning into a nation of information addicts and the majority of people are unaware of the level to which they feed their addiction.

When used in a positive way technology can give you the flexibility and freedom you desire. It's all about achieving balance and making it work for you. To do this you need to assess your situation, the impact technology has had on your life, how you use it and whether your stress levels are reaching an unmanageable state.

▪ Time Management

Time management is the key to getting it right, but it is important to define just what that means. When life is spiralling out of control we chase time in a way that always keeps it beyond reach.

Think of a three-minute task. When I ask my clients to do this, I get some very amusing answers, but common ones include making a cup of tea or boiling an egg. Technically correct, but if you intend drinking the tea and eating the egg the task obviously takes longer. Look at your own task and think about *all* the processes involved. We often measure tasks this way, making no allowances for preparation, interruptions and the sort of person we are.

You could be the sort of person who puts the kettle on and sits down to read the newspaper. The kettle clicks off and you keep reading. Eventually you get round to making the tea, but the whole process has now taken 20 minutes. Or you could be working, making a phone call, attending to children and trying to fit in another task. Fitting in other tasks isn't the problem, but trying to fit in too many is. At the end of the day you may have tackled lots of jobs, but still be left with a list of mostly incomplete tasks.

Doing this on a regular basis is a big stress trigger. It leaves you feeling you never get ahead; in fact you can't even get to the finishing post. You may be wondering what this has to do with technology – well, unless you learn to handle time, don't look to technology to provide the answers. It just becomes another item on the list, something else you have to juggle.

Don't Tell Me You're Busy

Planning your time allows you to do the things you want to do as well as the things you have to do. The pace of life means you have to be organised. Have you noticed how organised people don't make a point of telling you how busy they are? Disorganised people do. They spend their day rushing from one thing to the next, they are always late for appointments – telephone them and they are too busy to talk to you. These could be symptoms of real overload, but the disorganised individual is easily overloaded because they are creating their own chaos rather than being subjected to it.

Overload is a genuine condition that can creep up on you without you realising it, until the physical and psychological effects start to take over. But it's important to know how much of the problem is external and how much is of your own making. Run through the checklist below to see where you are. Be honest and don't let your ego get in the way. Ego is that voice in your head that wants to make your life an exception. It tells you that you don't have a problem with time management, but rather your life really is much busier than everyone else's. The following list will identify if you are disorganised. Put a tick next to anything that applies to you:

- You are constantly late for appointments ☐

- You regularly lose things, such as paperwork, keys, telephone numbers ☐

- You leave bills unopened or pile them into a drawer ☐

- You don't return phone calls or are slow to do so ☐

- You often forget things ☐

- You frequently miss deadlines ☐

- People are always chasing you for work ☐

- You feel anxious and stressed most of the day ☐

- When you go to bed your mind is racing with things to do ☐

- There are piles of paperwork on your desk ☐

- You create mess and clutter ☐

- You take on lots of tasks, but rarely complete them ☐

- You have a limited attention span and are regularly accused of not listening ☐

- You go to bed much later than you would like to ☐

- You find it difficult to relax and switch off ☐

- You frequently tell people how busy you are ☐

- You can't remember what you watched on TV last night or what you read in the newspaper ☐

- You are in the habit of saying 'Can you tell me that later?' ☐

Most of us could tick a few things on this list, but any more than five and your life needs some serious reorganisation. So here are some simple techniques to implement change.

Improve your time management skills

► Prioritise your priorities. Make a daily list of the tasks you have to do and a commitment to completing them. Finishing 90 per cent of the task won't do because all those 1 per cents add up to one big headache.

► Clear your clutter at home and at work.

► Set yourself realistic time-frames. If you are always running late your perception of time is out of synch, so start timing how long things take.

► Set aside at least 10 minutes every day for time out. This is when you do nothing and I mean nothing. No TV, radio, reading or music – just sit quietly and clear your mind by concentrating on your breathing.

► Keep a daybook or journal. This should include a list of things to do each day and where you are at with each one. So if you make a phone call, make a few notes on the outcome – do you have to call back, send a letter, wait to hear back from them. Don't rely on memory.

► Don't book unnecessary meetings when a phone call, e-mail or letter would be just as acceptable.

► Always establish the purpose of a meeting before booking one or, where possible, attending one.

► Learn to say no and accept that you are doing no one any favours, least of all yourself, when you over-commit.

► Your time is valuable, so don't waste other people's by getting back to them and detailing how busy you are. Trust me, they don't want to hear your itinerary.

► Not returning phone calls sends out signals that you are rude, inefficient and disrespectful of other people's time. Make a point of dealing with your messages on a daily basis. The same applies to e-mails.

► Have a good filing system and file your paperwork each day.

▪ Technology at Work

We are still a youthful IT economy that has invested highly in the promised benefits of technology, mainly increased productivity. Yet economists are debating what has been termed the 'productivity paradox'. Robert Kling, Professor of Information Science at Indiana University, says: 'There has been a relentless promotion of computerisation as almost guaranteeing large productivity gains at work. But the economy doesn't bear that out.' Professor Pete Makin of UMIST has researched behaviour in e-mail use and reports that 'When they arrive, people find reading them more pleasurable than working, so it's a good excuse to leave what they're doing.'

So, how can it be that so many workers find they are working longer and harder when productivity doesn't support this? There have been reports on the millions of pounds businesses lose through staff playing PC games, the amount of time lost e-mailing friends and forwarding jokes, and excessively accessing information. While this would account for loss I don't believe that technology is creating an entire workforce that would rather shirk work than shift it.

From the evidence I see the majority of workers are trying to get to grips with using technology in a productive way. But its introduction has been incredibly fast. In an ideal world, we would have had more time to balance the old way of working with the new way. Many organisations have made extreme changes to the way staff work, virtually eliminating much of the social interaction and face-to-face communication that previously existed. Along with this, many of the aspects of work that individuals found satisfying have gone, like having more control, receiving personal feedback, applying skills in a variety of ways and seeing more tangible evidence of completed work. All this can make some areas of work feel fragmented. There are also technical blips to contend with and you can't take your terminal aside for a cup of coffee and a heart-to-heart when it throws your day into chaos.

Technology itself isn't the problem or enemy. We are all experiencing growing pains as it is integrated into our working lives. Disadvantages that were not easy to predict are only now revealing themselves. And it's a learning process for both employer and employee.

▪ Using the Formula to Avoid Technological Overload

Knowing the warning signs allows you to take action before the situation becomes unmanageable. Work through the Formula to find out if technological overload affects you and what sort of action you need to take.

Focus

For this exercise, you need to think about how technology has affected and changed the way you work. Make a detailed list in your journal of all the different types of technology you use at work – e-mail, Internet, voice mail, computers and so on. Then answer the following questions:

1. Has technology made your working life easier or more difficult?

2. Has your volume of work increased?

3. Does technology allow you to be more productive or less productive?

4. Do you feel technology works for you and you are the master of it, or do you feel like the slave to it?

5. Is your work life more stressful or less stressful than it used to be?

Organise

Using technology effectively can make you appear productive and organised. But if you are disorganised technology is just a more advanced way to waste time. You know what your working day consists of – warning signs include:

► being an e-mail junkie with a large percentage of the e-mails you send or receive being non-work related

► losing hours every day playing PC games

► trying out all the IT systems available just because they're there

► creating non-productive work to relieve the boredom

► not prioritising or limiting the amount of time you spend getting information

► staring at your computer screen, unable to work unless it prompts you to do so.

If you are already organised, then you need to think about any other problems that technology is causing you; for example, is there too much information coming through, with not enough time to process or log the information you receive? Is there an unmanageable workload? Are there too many interruptions? It may even be that you are trying to use a system or software package that is supposed to work in theory but definitely not in practice. So you need to identify when the problem really is technology based and not personal disorganisation.

Review

This is the time to review how the problem affects you and the level of stress you are experiencing. In this context the word stress refers to what's outside your level of comfort. Extreme symptoms include feeling overwhelmed on a regular basis, resorting to alcohol or drug abuse, an inability to focus and concentrate, increased sickness and absenteeism. Staff can be reluctant to complain about technology overload and think it is a weakness on their part. I hope I can alleviate any fears you may have by telling you that overload is a real problem, not an imaginary or subjective one. Not everyone will experience the same stress, so you are the best person to monitor the effects and impact it has on you.

Motivate

Finding a solution will motivate you and you certainly won't feel motivated by procrastinating. There can be a real temptation to distract yourself with e-mails, the Internet and PC games. But this won't keep you motivated and these time-wasting distractions are of no more use to you than they are to your employer. Work soon feels unfulfilling and monotonous, which leads to stress. Motivate yourself by monitoring your own productivity – you could find, for example, that instead of an e-mail or online transaction, a certain amount of face-to-face communication secures better relationships and is more productive. At least by exploring different options you can put forward a good case to your employer if you are achieving results. Remember, employers have installed systems to increase productivity and are usually very open to ideas that improve it.

Utilise

Technology has many benefits when used properly. But one of the fastest ways to overload is overuse and it can be very easy to rely on it too much and not utilise your other skills. You need variety and, even if your strengths are in the IT area, there may still be other skills you have, such as interpersonal ones. Review the skills audit you did in Chapter 7 and look for ways to incorporate the other skills you listed into your working day.

Liberate

If you are suffering from overload and stress now is the time to consider what you can let go of. How much of the technology you use at work is compulsory? Do you really have to use it as much as you are? Even implementing small changes can make a big difference, like turning off your mobile for an hour a day, making sure you take a break from your screen and physically move away from it, limiting all non-relevant and time-consuming e-mails. You may believe that your work would suffer and you would be less efficient, but you can't know for sure until you try. And when you are stressed you are nowhere near as productive as you think. Being stressed makes every task feel like hard work and no one likes to go home feeling exhausted when they have been non-productive. But that's exactly what happens, because you are running on pure nervous energy which, over time, undermines your performance.

Act

It's time to take action. There are lots of things you can do – try speaking to your employer or your colleagues – there is strength in numbers, and if you are feeling overwhelmed and stressed, you probably aren't the only one. So, why not take responsibility for getting the ball rolling? Your action could begin with getting a medical to see if you are suffering from work-related hazards like eyestrain or repetitive strain injury (RSI), stress, exhaustion and burnout. You might decide that you have to be more disciplined about how you use technology, which can be addictive and habit forming. It can be a revelation to wean yourself away from some of it and find that much of what you use just isn't necessary.

Now you have identified any problems along with what action you can take, it's time to 'face' the challenge. Refer back to Chapter 1 if you need a quick reminder of what to do.

▪ Technology in the Home

Would you say your home life is significantly different from your work life? It can be useful to find out. Much of your working day involves dealing with a great deal of information, especially when you are using a lot of technology. Overload comes from too much information and you may be surprised just how much that process continues outside of work. TV is a popular choice of relaxation for a large percentage of people. So much so that they can spend as many hours in front of the box as they do at work. While it may seem like a good way to switch off, it's easy to overlook the amount of information they are exposed to at the same time. Not just in the form of the programmes, but all the advertising. Thousands of messages are bombarded at viewers, even in a few hours.

Then there are all the other activities we see as relaxation. Sitting down to read a newspaper or our favourite magazine means more information, more adverts, more overload. The weekend newspapers are bigger than the daily ones and the number of supplements is constantly increasing to include all the additional technology guides like TV guides, Internet and computer guides, with the latest gadgets and upgrades available. Before you know it every minute of your waking day is invaded with information.

Silence starts to feel like an unnatural state. Do you wake up and instantly turn on the TV or radio? Or jump in the car and switch on the radio as automatically as the engine? Or keep your mobile glued to your side, or spend hours on the Internet? Perhaps one of the most alarming things is that you are probably unaware you are doing this.

Just because something becomes the norm doesn't mean we have really adapted to it. This is all new territory and we have entered it at a very fast pace. The great myth is that we have all this additional choice about how we spend our free time. But do we? Surely what we actually have is just lots more ways to overload ourselves with information. We may have the appearance of choice, in that we can choose how we access it, but whatever choice we make we are still getting the same end result: information, information and more information.

So, where is our switch-off point? When do we know when we're had enough? Unfortunately, all too frequently we don't and only respond to the symptoms of having too much.

When Alex came to see me he explained that he needed help organising his time. 'I'm a very busy person and don't have time to organise my day properly so I thought I'd get a coach to do it for me.' Then he continued, 'Sure, run the figures by me and I'll let you know if I'm interested.' I thought he had taken leave of his senses until I spotted his mobile ear-piece and realised he was taking a call. When I insisted on him turning off his mobile so he could focus on our conversation you would have thought I had suggested turning off his life-support system from his look of horror. As soon as the session was over he immediately checked it.

Alex found it a difficult session. He had the misplaced idea that a coach can take over your life and organise it for you and show you how to cram more things into an already overloaded schedule. Alex was setting his own unmanageable pace and would not review the possibility he was trying to do too much. His job in the City involved long hours, he was setting up a couple of businesses on the side and his hectic social life kept him out every evening.

Alex kept insisting he had lots of energy and could keep up the pace, although all the signs indicated otherwise. He talked quickly, was always interrupting, was not good at listening and found it hard retaining information. He also had problems sleeping and would watch TV into the early hours. His mobile phone never left his side and, as much of his business dealing was abroad, he was on 24-hour alert.

At this meeting Alex wasn't listening to me. His new coach was confronting him with issues he just didn't want to deal with.

It was three months before I heard from Alex again, and it was a very different and liberated man I met with at our next session. He had left his job in the City rather than face being demoted. 'This firm can do without butterfly mentalities holding senior positions', had been the harsh words from his boss. Unbeknown to Alex his firm had been monitoring him for several months, and had noted the number of non-work related calls and e-mails he made and received, his erratic behaviour and his inability to follow tasks through. He was lucky not to have been sacked. The sideline businesses had fallen through and his phone had stopped ringing. This was not the time for 'I *did* warn you', because it was a real pleasure to see the newly focused Alex. Going back to the drawing board had meant reviewing and re-evaluating his values and making a personal commitment to priorities.

Alex was about to start a new job as financial controller for a small chain of retail outlets. It was a good job, the firm was less competitive than his previous one and he wasn't expected to work long hours. He was excited about his new position, but his time away from work had given him the chance to pursue other interests. Alex had bought a dog and was enjoying long country walks with his new chum. He was relaxed, healthier, sleeping well and feeling great.

While work was still important, so were the other areas of his life. Using the standard coaching forms I encouraged Alex to set goals in every area. His focus and commitment was to achieve a work/life balance, which he is acting on and well on the way to doing.

I wanted to tell you about Alex because a coach isn't a fairy godmother and Cinderella won't meet her deadline of midnight if she's attending several balls that evening. Life in the fast lane has an intoxicating appeal, but you have to know when to draw the line. This requires you having a sense of direction, to know what your goals are and what it is you want to achieve. Otherwise, you will be pulled all over the place and what you think is direction is actually distraction. Alex was on the lookout for opportunity, but he wasn't channelling his energies. The result was that they became fragmented. In situations like this there is no follow-through because you are so busy racing ahead of yourself that there is no time to stop and take stock of the situation.

Some people respond to the warning signs in life. For others it takes a major collision before taking stock. For these individuals, sooner or later something has to give, whether it's your health, job, relationships or social life. Even a computer will crash on overload. But it doesn't have to be like this. You are capable of managing every aspect of your life. The key, of course, is balance.

If you jumped in your car and started driving with no proper destination or plan of where you were going, you'd expect to wind up lost. But that's just what a lot of people do in their approach to work. Having a route or plan doesn't mean life has to be predictable or dull. It simply means you know where you are going, there are lots of routes you can take and you can also stop off along the way to make sure you are going in the right direction.

Keeping yourself constantly occupied, entertained and busy using technology is not how you switch off, especially if that's how much of your working day is spent. The ease with which technology has entered our homes can encourage habit-forming patterns. Accessing it requires little effort or forward planning. But, ultimately, we may not be doing something outside working hours that is substantially different enough and allows us to achieve a healthy balance. Variety is a powerful way to counteract stress.

▪ Being Selective

'Everything in moderation', as the old saying goes. It may be a cliché, but of course it's absolutely true. Too much of anything is what leads to problems, and that is never more true than in the case of managing time and technology.

The new information highway has done away with much of the exclusiveness of gaining knowledge. We haven't all gone to the best schools, valued education during our formative years, or been provided with opportunity and encouragement. I'm a firm believer in how empowering knowledge is and the difference it can make to your life. You are probably waiting for a 'but' or 'however' – not this time. You are in a better position than ever before to have the sort of life you want. The information you need is at hand. To begin with we are all like kids in a sweetshop, grabbing everything in sight. What seem like time-saving methods soon become time-consuming when you aren't selective. For example, you can use the Internet for home shopping, financial services, insurance, buying property, booking holidays and much more. But there wouldn't be much point in accessing these services if you didn't make use of them.

Technology is seductive and it's fun to try out the latest gadget or service. But don't spend hours downloading more information than you actually need. You may not have as much choice about the impact of technology at work as you would like, but you certainly have choice in the rest of your life. Try some forward planning and time restrictions. Use the following guidelines:

► Restrict the number of hours you watch TV. Check out programmes in advance and choose what you want to watch.

► Unless you are part of the emergency services your mobile doesn't have to be constantly switched on. If you are at the point where you can't leave home without it, you are not giving yourself the time out you need.

► Set aside time every day to take stock of your day. Have you achieved what you set out to? Are you trying to do too much? How can you improve on things tomorrow?

► Review how you spend your leisure time. Does it involve pursuits that give you face to face contact with other people? Are you spending time maintaining and improving relationships with those you care most about? Are you watching TV to numb out from an overloaded day? Do you seek to be entertained and occupied every minute of the day? Build into your day periods of relaxation, even if they are very brief ones.

► Add variety to your leisure activities and ensure they are substantially different from your working activities.

▪ Facing the Challenge

You should now be ready to 'face' the challenge.

(**F**ormula + **A**pplication + **C**hange + **E**xperience) = **results**

You applied the Formula earlier in this chapter to see how technology at work was affecting you. You have also thought about its use in the home. Decide what would be the best action or actions for you to take. These can involve finding more varied ways of working that allow you to use other skills, limiting the time you spend gathering information on non-essential tasks. In the home you should be looking for variety in leisure activities, time out and pursuits that encourage interpersonal and face-to-face communication. From applying new ways of doing things you want to see positive changes like reduced stress levels, better focus and concentration, and feeling calmer and more relaxed. Record all new experiences in your journal, so that you can determine when you are achieving the results you desire.

▪ Coaching Review

► Technology can provide you with flexibility and freedom when you use it the right way.

► Learn to manage your time properly and don't expect technology to provide all the answers.

► Organised people don't make a point of telling you how busy they are.

► Check for the warning signs of being disorganised.

► Implement simple changes to reorganise your life.

► Monitor the amount of time you spend using technology at work and how productive you actually are.

► Look for a variety of ways to apply your skills, rather than finding ways to distract yourself or relieve boredom.

► Look out for signs of stress, such as feeling overwhelmed, increased sickness and absenteeism, alcohol or drug abuse, inability to focus and concentrate.

► Don't get in the habit of gathering and accessing information for the sake of it. Be clear about what you want to achieve from it and make selective choices.

► Your home life needs to be substantially different from your working life as this will help you relax and unwind – this may require you to limit technology use for recreation.

► Finally – you can only make a difference by taking action.

CHAPTER ELEVEN

Achieving a Work/Life Balance

ALTHOUGH THIS IS A book about achieving success at work, it would not be complete without considering what success means, what price you pay for it, and how to balance the demands of a career with the rest of your life.

Letting your life get out of balance is more common than you may think – and more serious. You may believe you can put areas of your life on hold and attend to them at a later date. Becoming totally preoccupied with one area of life can blinker you from the damage you may be inflicting on other areas.

Initially you may not notice minor health problems, or that personal relationships seem more distant. Finances taking a turn for the worse can be written off as a 'blip', as can dwindling social engagements, weakening family bonds and failing to acknowledge religious or spiritual convictions. But those 'minor problems' are signals of something far more serious. Before you know it, they're running out of control, and you wake up one day and wonder how your life got so seriously out of balance. Don't wait for a crisis before you take action.

Several years ago I lay virtually paralysed, awaiting major spinal surgery. For months – even years – before I had ignored niggling health problems and work overload as I forged ahead with my career. Work had dominated much of my life and I was paying a high price for neglecting the rest of it. It was a turning point, and there were powerful and painful lessons to be learnt. Not least of all was having to deal with an ego that relied so heavily on the rank and position I held at work. I was the boss, the person in charge and felt so secure with my status I had become complacent about the other areas of my life and the people who were part of them. I failed to give them the attention and respect they deserved.

Achieving success at work can be deeply rewarding and if it's your goal it is well worth striving for. But it doesn't have to be at the expense of the rest of your life. In fact, if you want to be happy and fulfilled as well as successful, it's crucial that it isn't.

Never forget that no matter what level of success you achieve there are no guarantees that things will stay as they are. Careers can have fallow periods, your goals and ambitions may change.

▪ The Seven Steps

If you have devoted everything to work, where does that leave you? My career crisis was temporary and something I could rebuild. The biggest challenge was getting the rest of my life in order and the whole process would have been far less painful if I hadn't ignored the importance of achieving a work/life balance. It was during this time that I developed the foundation for my coaching programme and a new way of balancing my own life. I identified seven major life areas, which I refer to as the seven steps. They are as follows.

1. Health

2. Spiritual/religious life

3. Work/career

4. Financial

5. Personal relationships

6. Family/extended family

7. Friends/social life

In this chapter I will be showing you how to set goals for each of the seven steps and balance your work life with these other important areas.

EXERCISE
Life Chart

Fill in the life chart below to establish how you are feeling right now. Give yourself a score for each area, by ringing the appropriate number. If you're feeling really miserable and discontent give yourself a 1, if you couldn't be happier, put a score that reflects that.

	Low									*High*
• Health	1	2	3	4	5	6	7	8	9	10
• Spiritual/religious life	1	2	3	4	5	6	7	8	9	10
• Work/career	1	2	3	4	5	6	7	8	9	10
• Financial	1	2	3	4	5	6	7	8	9	10
• Personal relationships	1	2	3	4	5	6	7	8	9	10
• Family/extended family	1	2	3	4	5	6	7	8	9	10
• Friends/social life	1	2	3	4	5	6	7	8	9	10

You can use the above scores to monitor your progress as we work through each of the seven steps.

• The Coaching Forms

In the Appendix you will find seven separate forms for each of the seven steps. You can use these or complete your own on A4 size paper and keep them in a folder. These are identical to the forms I use for one-to-one coaching with clients. In Chapter 3 I explained how to complete each section, but I'll run through it again now to remind you. Although the sections on each form are numbered, you are not limited to the amount you fill in for each section, so you can have more than three goals, personal strengths, development skills and so on.

Goals

List the things you want to achieve. Your goals must be positive and relate to you. For example, in the family section it's better to write 'I want to improve my relationship with my daughter', rather than 'I want my daughter to treat me better.' The second example puts the onus of responsibility on your daughter to achieve the goal, when it should be on you. Here are some examples of goals for each of the seven steps:

1. **Health** Take more exercise

2. **Spiritual/religious life** Practise my religion/beliefs

3. **Work/career** Apply for a new job in the next month

4. **Financial** Invest in a pension scheme

5. **Personal relationships** Communicate better with my partner and be more honest

6. **Family/extended family** Spend more quality time with my family

7. **Friends/social life** Contact my friends more often and arrange to see them regularly

Personal Strengths

List your strengths, not your weaknesses. These will remind you of all the attributes you have to help you achieve your goals. Here are examples of the sort of strengths to include:

1. **Health** I am committed to taking care of my body

2. **Spiritual/religious life** My beliefs encourage me to be tolerant and forgiving to others

3. **Work/career** I am highly skilled and have excellent references

4. **Financial** I am good at saving money

5. **Personal relationships** I am ready to make a commitment to my partner

6. **Family/extended family** I always make time for my family

7. **Friends/social life** I am a loyal and supportive friend

Immediate Challenges/Blocks/Problems

Focus on how a problem directly affects you and don't blame or pass the problem to someone else. Stating 'My mother-in-law is difficult', for example, is not describing the problem in a way that allows you to find a solution. Better to say 'I have a problem with how my mother-in-law treats me' or 'I need to have boundaries with my mother-in-law.' Bringing the problem back to you and changing the way you describe it is the first step to overcoming a block.

1. **Health** I want to take more exercise but am not good at self-discipline

2. **Spiritual/religious life** My behaviour is not in line with my beliefs

3. **Work/career** I am not fulfilling my full potential

4. **Financial** My overdraft is spiralling out of control

5. **Personal relationships** I'm afraid to get into a relationship in case I get hurt

6. **Family/extended family** I allow my family to interfere in my life

7. **Friends/social life** I don't make enough time for my friends

Development Skills

Increasing and developing new skills will help you achieve your goals. So, if your goal in a personal relationship is to communicate better with your partner, good development skills would be learning to listen and express your feelings without criticising your partner. Here are some other examples to get you started:

1. **Health** Learn how to do yoga

2. **Spiritual/religious life** Be more accepting of other people's beliefs

3. **Work/career** Enrol on a computer course

4. **Financial** Be more responsible for my finances

5. **Personal relationships** Be more supportive to my partner

6. **Family/extended family** Communicate my boundaries

7. **Friends/social life** Make the effort to get to know new people

Achievements

Most people focus more on what they haven't achieved, rather than what they have achieved. Reminding yourself of your achievements gets you in the frame of mind of a successful individual. Successful people don't focus on their failures or any lack of progress, as they are tuned into making the most of all the personal resources they have. This keeps you on the lookout for new opportunities. Don't underestimate or overlook the skills you have and what they have allowed you to achieve. If you are a first-time job seeker with no work experience and the position you have applied for requires someone trustworthy who can take responsibility, there could be another area in your life chart with an achievement that demonstrates these qualities. For example, were you head boy or girl at school, treasurer at the tennis club, or an organiser and fundraiser of charity events? Other examples might include:

1. **Health** I have an excellent level of physical fitness and stamina

2. **Spiritual/religious life** I have become a better person by following my beliefs

3. **Work/career** I received the best appraisal in my department

4. **Financial** I have never been in debt

5. **Personal relationships** I have a secure and happy relationship

6. **Family/extended family** I have a wonderful relationship with my family

7. **Friends/social life** I have never lost touch with good friends and see them regularly

Filling in Your Forms

Now it's time to start filling in your forms. You need to set aside time to do this and keep referring back to the examples I have provided to make sure you are filling in your forms properly. Whenever you set a negative goal you will remain blocked. For instance, a common goal in the health chart is to lose weight. This is negative and keeps your focus on the problem (excess weight) rather than the outcome (getting in shape). Simply changing your goal to getting in shape switches your focus to ways in which you can do this. Every time you set a goal ask yourself, 'Am I stating what I want as an outcome or am I describing the problem?'. Here are some examples of positive and negative goals.

	POSITIVE GOALS	**NEGATIVE GOALS**
Health	Get in shape	Lose weight
Spiritual/ religious life	Teach my children about their religion	Make my children follow their religion
Work/career	Get a promotion	Stop being overlooked for promotion
Financial	Improve my financial position	Get out of debt
Personal relationships	Communicate my needs to my partner	Make my partner understand me
Family/ extended family	Set clear boundaries	Stop my family interfering
Friends/social life	Spend time with friends I like	Get rid of the friends I no longer enjoy being with

As you can see – the negative goals highlight the problem, not the solution. Some of them are also 'manipulative goals', whereby you are imposing your wishes on another person. Goals should not be about 'making' another person do something. You can't *make* someone understand you or want the things you want. Equally, you can't give others the responsibility of achieving the goal for you.

Of course, there will be lots of times when you have joint and shared goals with others. Close personal relationships require a sharing of core values and certain goals are fundamental to the success of that relationship. Finding a partner with similar core values is part of the synchronicity we all seek in relationships. But it's important to recognise that your goals are personal and some are only relevant to you.

Here are some more guidelines for each of the seven steps.

Improve your health

Having a healthy body and mind is fundamentally important. This underpins your quality of life generally, and is also what enables you to achieve your goals.

Set goals you believe are achievable and are going to stick to. It's better to start with small changes, like using the stairs instead of the lift, or drinking a fruit juice instead of another gin and tonic. Fitting in an exercise routine needs sensible planning, so if long working hours and overtime is your norm take this into account. Trips to the gym can be scheduled for weekends or buying an exercise video gives you flexibility as to when you use it. We don't all enjoy the same types of exercise and working up a sweat in the gym may not be your thing. When goals feel like an effort you will find plenty of excuses not to follow through on them. Making time for what you enjoy is much easier.

Use your health form to integrate changes that fit with your lifestyle rather than trying to make changes that require major lifestyle reorganising. There are seven life areas to balance and the best way to do it is one step at a time.

Discover your spirituality

For many people there is a connection between their value system and spiritual and religious convictions. Commercial goals can be pursued without abandoning your core values and beliefs. You need to know what these are to avoid creating a conflict between the two.

This is an optional area in my coaching programme, but regardless of how significant it is in your life you should still give it some thought. Even if you consider yourself a non-religious person, you may have ethics and beliefs that are spiritual in nature.

A useful exercise is seeing how your values align with the beliefs you have. Compare the goals you have set to the values and beliefs you have to see if they are compatible. Think about the various options available. Perhaps the goal is OK and the block has been in how you would achieve it. For example, perhaps the goal is to make money, but to make money in your existing employment requires you to be ruthlessly competitive. This behaviour could be out of line with your values. The goal of making money may still be OK – you'll just need to find another way of achieving it. There are a number of reasons why individuals fail to achieve their goals, but one of the most common is setting goals that compromise values and beliefs.

Get the most from your work and career

You have already completed much of what has to done in this area by assessing your current job, finding out what you really want from it and the choices you have. Now it's time to put these in context with the rest of your life and relationships.

The rest of this book has mainly focused on this area in isolation. When you have completed all your forms you should review them collectively. Problems in one area definitely impact on other areas. By reviewing all the seven steps together, you can develop a big-picture perspective on your life. You now know the value work has in your life; it could be greater or less than when you started this book. Even where it remains a great passion, never forget that there are still other areas to balance it with.

This chapter is about achieving a work/life balance, so this is the time to determine if the goals you have set in your work chart accommodate the goals in the rest of your life charts. I know lots of people who would love to spend more time with their family, but have become so caught up in the career treadmill that they never jump off. They are running towards one goal, but away from another one. Sometimes ambition or money drives the treadmill. At the end of the day you have decide what you value the most. Don't misunderstand me on this point, however. For example, having a family means supporting a family and you need money to do that. Perspective comes from deciding how much money is enough. Is it once you are in a position to take care of the basics? Or, when you achieve this do you want more for your family, such as a better house, education, holidays and so on? Making the right choices involves getting your priorities in place and that requires you to consider the impact decisions will have on every area of your life. There is nothing more frustrating than to think you have made the wrong choice for all the right reasons.

Trying to balance the situation in your head is crazy-making stuff. That's why this pen-and-paper exercise is so valuable. Time and time again clients tell me what a revealing process the forms are. It allows them to see the bigger picture, how easy it is to get life out of balance and most significantly how solutions reveal themselves when they are no longer scrambling all the information in their heads.

Achieving that balance is about contributing to every area collectively. Of course, you can't always balance everything equally all the time. Some days a family crisis may take all your time and attention, while on another an urgent work project may fully occupy you. However, by referring to your forms on a weekly basis you can review the situation and remain aware of any areas that are being neglected or receiving too much time and attention overall.

Sort out your finances

In Chapter 7 we looked at your basic relationship to money and financial goals. As a follow-on there will be techniques on practical budgeting and more goal-setting exercises to achieve results in this area.

How much money is enough? My high-earning clients worry as much about money as those in a much lower income bracket.

As with every aspect of coaching I bring the question back to the client. It's for them to decide how much money is enough, what they spend their money on and how they manage their finances. Ask yourself the following questions:

- How much money is enough?

- Am I happy with my current financial status?

- Do I enjoy my money?

- Am I ready to take responsibility for my finances?

- Is my financial position improving or declining?

- Do I spend beyond my means?

- Do I manage to save money?

These questions will help you set goals and identify any problems and blocks. When you have goals in place you know what you are working to and for. You can also take action to prevent repeating any negative patterns, like spending beyond your means. If you are saving money, remind yourself regularly why and what it is you want to achieve. Positive financial goals include:

▶ increasing my earning potential

▶ saving 10 per cent of my annual income

▶ saving up to go on holiday

▶ working to a monthly budget.

Enrich your personal relationships

This is where you will focus on what you want from a relationship, bringing the right relationships into your life, setting goals, dealing with your emotions and making the right decisions to secure your happiness.

Even when we have very good personal relationships we can become complacent and take them for granted. Setting goals stops you only attending to this area when there is a problem or crisis. Every relationship has to be worked at and we often overlook our closest ones. When I see clients who are happy with their relationships, the best goal they can come up with is usually 'Continue to have a happy relationship', which does have an element of complacency about it. A more aspirational goal would be to improve a relationship rather than simply maintain it.

You do have to be really honest about what you want from a personal relationship. This can be quite a challenge. Deep down you always know when you are not getting what you want, but there can be a lot of fear about rocking the boat. For some reason – no one really knows why – writing down a goal is far more likely to prompt you into taking action. If the real goal was, say, to get married and have children, a make-do goal would be 'To continue the relationship'. The make-do goal, which is denying what we really want, feels safer because you are not confronting the real issue. When the real goal is identified you may have to face up to the fact that the relationship you are in is not going to give you what you want. Getting what you want could involve making a painful decision. But the right decision will not always be the easiest one. You will only take action when you are ready to. But doing nothing is not the way to achieve goals.

Develop your relationship with your family and extended family

This is about how to get on with those people whom fate, not friendship, chose for you. This will involve setting boundaries, improving family bonds and dealing with any unresolved issues that are keeping you blocked.

For example, balancing work life and family life continues to be a challenge for the majority of women. Society sends out such mixed signals when women are told they can have it all and then are made to feel guilty for trying to.

What's becoming more evident in recent years is that men are also becoming more concerned about the effect of long working hours on the family. While many still are keen to pursue a career, the days are gone when they will do so at any cost. The positive aspect to come out of this is that when both men and women join forces on this issue more pressure is put on employers to accommodate the needs of family life. In the past career opportunities were snapped up by men who were in a better position to work long, unsociable hours. Today employers are having to rethink the demands they make on employees, because regardless of financial rewards the level of dissatisfaction in this area indicates this is no compensation for the high price employees pay: the loss of balance in their lives.

Achieving your family goals can require you to make changes to your working life. Simply wanting to spend more time with your family isn't going to happen if you continue working very long hours. Increased flexibility is making its way into the workplace because employers need to retain good staff, so it's well worth getting information on what's out there. Technology allows home working, and there are growing numbers of companies who offer term-time contracts, childcare, job sharing and employee assistance programmes (EAPs). Working for a family friendly firm is definitely going to improve your prospects of achieving a healthy balance.

The family/extended family form can also be used to put boundaries in place. Family relationships commonly break down, so use this form to set goals about the sort of boundaries you want and to tackle any unresolved issues.

Work on your friendships and social life

Your friendships and social life should enrich your life. As our lives and circumstances change, friendships change too. You need to assess which friends will help you move forward and which ones have a vested interest in holding you back. This should be done in conjunction with techniques to improve and develop your social life.

Friendships developed at work are valuable relationships and may spill over into social life. But if you or a colleague changes job it can become evident that the overriding connection was your mutual employment. Take this away and the friendship can lose much of the glue that held it together. Suddenly you have far less in common with that friend.

Of course, some friendships are capable of standing the test of time and change – whatever the circumstances – but not all friendships. It can feel painful and confusing when friends change. We tell ourselves, 'It's not that we don't want to see them making progress – it's just that we like them the way they are.' When you make changes in your own life you will find that some friends are more able to embrace this than others. It can feel unfair – after all, aren't friends supposed to accept us the way we are? Unfortunately, this is not always the reality and they may not like the new terms of friendship.

For example, picture a friendship where a huge amount of your social life has been spent with a particular friend. Then you start a relationship and have to divide time between your new partner and your friend. Then you get married and have a family, your work hours increase, your priorities change and you have less time to spend with your friend. Your friend is not getting what they used to from the relationship and, chances are, neither are you.

When relationships change it doesn't have to be a signal for them to end. My close friend singer-songwriter Lynsey de Paul provided one of my favourite analogies of friendship. She compares them to the colours of the rainbow, with each colour representing something different a friend has to offer. Some friends have more than one colour to offer, some have just one colour and along the way colours change. So long as they never move into the grey they have a place in your life. Think about the friends you have and decide which ones still warrant a space in your life.

Is your social life all you would like it to be? If not, this is the time to address things and make some changes. Make sure that your goals are specific and detailed: if you want to go out more state where – the cinema, theatre, parties, nightclubs, dinner, hill walking? Gather information on forthcoming events that interest you and book in advance so you can plan your time. Aim for variety – the more diverse your activities are outside work the easier you will find it to switch off from work.

▪ The Formula for Achieving a Work/Life Balance

Here's a quick recap of the Formula to get you in solution mode. Follow the process all the way, through taking one problem at a time.

Focus

Think how the problem affects your life and how committed you are to finding a solution. Not all problems will prompt you to take action, so you have to be clear about the fact that you are actually prepared to follow through with a solution.

Organise

The vast majority of times we actually know the solution and don't act on it because of having other priorities, fear of change or the consequences, not wanting confrontation, being afraid of upsetting other people. List all possible solutions, even if they are ones you don't want to go with.

Review

Ask yourself the following questions:

- How long have you had this problem?

- How long are you likely to have it if you do nothing?

- Is that a pattern that keeps repeating?

- How does it affect other areas of your life?

- On a scale of one to ten (ten being severe), how unhappy/ stressed does the problem make you?

- How much time do you spend thinking about it?

Motivate

Answering the above questions will tell you if the problem really does warrant you doing something. Think about how much better you would feel not having this problem and the difference that it would make to your life.

Utilise

Make your strength your commitment to taking action.

Liberate

You will certainly feel liberated when you no longer have the problem. There may also be things you have to let go of in your life to make way for the changes you want to make.

Act

As always, you have to follow through with a solution by taking action.

▪ Facing the Challenge

With each of the seven steps you have to 'face' the challenge.

(Formula + Application + Change + Experience) = results

Tackling and changing every area at once is not a practical possibility. So, give yourself some deadlines to work to for each area:

1. **Health** I will improve my physical stamina over a six-month period

2. **Spiritual/religious life** I will set aside an hour every week for this area

3. **Work/career** I will apply for promotion in three months

4. **Finances** I will make an appointment to see an accountant at the end of the month

5. **Personal relationships** I will book a romantic weekend with my partner for the next Bank Holiday

6. **Family/extended family** I will telephone my parents every week

7. **Friends/social life** I will throw a party on my birthday and invite all my friends

▪ Coaching Review

This may seem like a wide-ranging chapter, but that's because life is wide ranging – or at least the healthiest and happiest lives are. Happiness and success can be achieved in every area. Working towards this is an ongoing process and I can't reiterate enough the consequences of ignoring any areas or thinking you can put them on hold.

▸ To achieve a work/life balance you have to give time and attention to each of the seven steps.

▪ And Finally

Well done! You've got to the end of this book. That means you're at the beginning – the beginning of a new way of life. Now you have mastered the Formula, it's there for you to apply whenever you need. And you can continue to use this book as a guide, referring back to it whenever you want to remind yourself of the techniques and exercises, or just for inspiration!

Now you are ready to face the challenge of achieving the work/life balance you desire. So, finally, let me wish you happiness and success in every area of your life.

The Forms

HEALTH

Goals

1

2

3

Personal Strengths

1

2

3

Immediate Challenges/Blocks/Problems

1

2

3

Development Skills

1

2

3

Achievements

1

2

3

SPIRITUAL

Goals

1

2

3

Personal Strengths

1

2

3

Immediate Challenges/Blocks/Problems

1

2

3

Development Skills

1

2

3

Achievements

1

2

3

WORK

Goals

1

2

3

Personal Strengths

1

2

3

Immediate Challenges/Blocks/Problems

1

2

3

Development Skills

1

2

3

Achievements

1

2

3

FINANCES

Goals

1

2

3

Personal Strengths

1

2

3

Immediate Challenges/Blocks/Problems

1

2

3

Development Skills

1

2

3

Achievements

1

2

3

PERSONAL RELATIONSHIPS

Goals

1

2

3

Personal Strengths

1

2

3

Immediate Challenges/Blocks/Problems

1

2

3

Development Skills

1

2

3

Achievements

1

2

3

FAMILY

Goals

1

2

3

Personal Strengths

1

2

3

Immediate Challenges/Blocks/Problems

1

2

3

Development Skills

1

2

3

Achievements

1

2

3

FRIENDS AND SOCIAL LIFE

Goals

1

2

3

Personal Strengths

1

2

3

Immediate Challenges/Blocks/Problems

1

2

3

Development Skills

1

2

3

Achievements

1

2

3

Further Reading

Dr Harry Alder, *Think Like a Leader* (Piatkus, 1995)

Nathaniel Branden, *How to Raise Your Self-Esteem* (Bantam, 1988)

Jack Canfield, Mark Victor Hansen, Maida Rogerson, Martin Rutte & Tim Clauss, *Chicken Soup for the Soul at Work* (Vermilion, 1999)

Richard Carlson, *Don't Sweat the Small Stuff at Work* (Hodder & Stoughton, 1999)

Roberta Cava, *Dealing with Difficult People* (Piatkus, 2000)

Jinny S. Ditzler, *Your Best Year Yet: Ten Questions for Making the Next Twelve Months Your Most Successful Ever* (Warner Books, 2000)

Louise L. Hay, *Heart Thoughts* (Eden Grove Editions, 1991)

Susan Jeffers, *The Little Book of Confidence* (Rider, 1999)

Susan Jeffers, *Feel the Fear and Do it Anyway* (Arrow, 1996)

Karen Mannering, *Managing Difficult People* (How to Books, 2000)

Andrew Matthews, *Being Happy: A Handbook to Greater Confidence and Security* (Price Stern Sloan, 1990)

Andrew Matthews, *Making Friends: A Guide to Getting Along With People* (Media Masters, 1990)

David Miln Smith & Sandra Leicester, *Hug the Monster* (Rider, 1997)

Eileen Mulligan, *Life Coaching: Change Your Life in 7 Days* (Piatkus, 1999)

Mitch Murray, *Mitch Murray's Handbook for the Terrified Speaker* (Foulsham, 1999)

Allan Pease, *Body Language* (Sheldon Press, 1984)

Sue Read, *Workshift* (Piatkus, 1999)

Anthony Robbins, *Awaken the Giant Within* (Simon & Schuster, 1992)

Brian Roet, *The Confidence to Be Yourself* (Piatkus, 1999)

Liz Simpson, *Working From the Heart* (Vermilion, 1999)

Hyrum W. Smith, *The 10 Natural Laws of Successful Time and Life Management* (Warner Books, 1994)

Cristina Stuart, *Speak for Yourself* (Piatkus, 2000)

Willet Weeks, *How to Get the Top Jobs That are Never Advertised* (Kogan Page, 1996)

Paul Wilson, *Calm at Work* (Penguin Books, 1998)

Bridget Wright, *Career Shift* (Piatkus, 1999)

Index